AMERICAN MULES

Martina Evans is an Irish poet and
novelist and the author of eleven books
of prose and poetry. *Now We Can Talk
Openly About Men* (Carcanet, 2018) –
an *Observer*, *Irish Times* and *TLS* Book
of the Year – it was also shortlisted
for the Roehampton Poetry Prize,
the *Irish Times* Poetry Now Award
and the Mark Pigott Poetry Prize.

# *American Mules*

## MARTINA EVANS

CARCANET

First published in Great Britain in 2021 by
Carcanet
Alliance House, 30 Cross Street
Manchester, M2 7AQ
www.carcanet.co.uk

A CIP catalogue record for this book is
available from the British Library.

ISBN 978 1 80017 089 6

Book design by Andrew Latimer
Printed in Great Britain by SRP Ltd, Exeter, Devon

The publisher acknowledges financial
assistance from Arts Council England.

# CONTENTS

## ACKNOWLEDGEMENTS

Thanks to the editors of the publications in which these poems of appeared:

*Poetry Review, PN Review, Poetry Ireland Review, London Magazine, The Irish Times, The Stinging Fly, The Lonely Crowd, Wales Arts Review, Rack Press, Enchanted Verses, Southword, bathmagg, Pratik, The Compass Magazine, The Tree Line: Poems for Trees, Woods & People,* Worple Press, 2017, *Washing Windows? Irish Women Write Poetry,* Arlen Press, 2017, *Reading the Future: New Writing from Ireland Celebrating 250 Years of Hodges Figgis,* Arlen House 2018, 'Oysters' was part of the art exhibition Please Do Not Touch at Studio Ex Purgamento, Camden, London in December 2015, 'Fine Gael form a Coalition Government with Labour, March 1973' was published as part of *The Writing Rights Project* which marked Human Rights Day 2015 in partnership with the Irish Times in December 2015. 'Seventy Seven' was commissioned by the Irish Literary Society in response to Michael Woods' Clarendon Lecture, *Yeats and Violence* at the Irish Embassy in London, 2019.

I wish to thank the Arts Council of England for a Grants for Arts Award which allowed me to continue to develop *Mountainy Men* in 2015. An earlier excerpt from *Mountainy Men* written in prose was published in the Irish Times in 2016. A big thank you to John McAuliffe who helped me to put two manuscripts together and not least Michael Schmidt for having faith in me.

*for Martin*

*over Edom will I cast out my shoe*
Psalms, 60:8

## HACKNEY TRIDENT

I think of Liam when I stand on a chair, shaking
as I should have been, considering what I found out afterwards –
that the fuse box didn't work. The current was
*running two ways in a loop –*
I think that was what the fourth electrician said.

It didn't trip for twenty years and I'd been worried
all that time if I'd remember how to wind the wire if it did trip
which it couldn't.

*Liam's all you can afford, Martina,* John was laughing.
He said the same about Spud Murph and
the amorous plumber.

Liam was very shook inside his too-big grey trousers, his legs
bending like ashplants, his grey stubble, the metallic sweet
smell of last night's alcohol,
hands trembling on the fixtures.

Will he take a cheque? *Jesus, if you offered Liam a cheque*
*he'd cry,* all of them squeezed into the van, waiting
for me to fork out so they could go.

*He's all you can afford, Martina.*

After Liam, the devout Catholic electrician's white eyebrows were
leaping,

*Did you know that washing machine had no earth? It's a disgrace for*
*any man to leave it that way*
*in a house with young girls.*

What about boys, middle-aged and old people?

*And that thing!*

The Hackney Trident, our 1920s cut-out
with its Jules Verne look and a habit of humming – a zzzzzzsssssing
so I didn't go down to it much.

When the devout Catholic died, his hitherto quiet side-kick
son turned up flaming drunk at 8.a.m.
*All right. All right. I know what I'm doing!*


Mick from UK Power Direct took it away in the end.
He said the Trident could be *very classy,* but he didn't
say my rusty, paint-splashed one was
although I still have a piece of its porcelain.

His parents were from Mayo and Kerry but he didn't say that
until we were alone.

I was lucky to have a Trident. If I was on
the other side of the road, I'd have
one of the Islington ones.

*We don't tell people we call them
Islington Deathboxes. You can't work on them live –
everything has to be off.*

And we didn't even have an earth, the old one
had rusted away back to Mother Earth.
Mick drilled a new one down.

The last time I tried John, he wasn't laughing.
He'd gone to collect Liam from his flat,
*The man was cold in his bed.* John, already
scared by his exploding oesophageal varices.

*I'd say he was there a while, Martina.*

SO

*for Mary Condé*

The best so was a *Now so!*
a triumphant there-you-are
which I tried out energetically
when wrapping a pan loaf
with the new peach-coloured tissue
that came in after
people realised that newsprint
mightn't be such a good idea
plastered on your bread.
*So sugaring what, you so-and-so!*
said Carol Carey before
complaining me to Mammy
for rolling six oranges over our black
wooden counter with my right hand
while reading from Maupassant
on my left. *I'll be on to your mother so!*
There was so as an alternative –
*I'm sorry, but we're out of Barry's Tea.*
*Well, I'll have Lyons's so.*
Or *I'll have Lyons's so then!*
Pale Ann Halloran came in
shyly, her arms folded,
no preliminary
only a heavy silence
before she said –
*I'll have a sliced pan so!*
when there had been no alternative
in the first place.
Like an answer without a question
it was a back-footed scene
so shrouded in ellipsis that

I couldn't speak –
especially when Anne was so shy too.
I didn't even get to wrap it.
The Keatings' green and white
and red and yellow
wax-papered sliced pan
was good to go –
so all that was left for me was
to say *Goodbye so!*
to Anne's pink woolen
retreating back
as I pitched coppers
and silver from a distance
of approximately six inches
into each wooden compartment
of the cash drawer
hoping they would land and
they rarely did –
just so.

# REGENCY PUMPS, CLONAKILTY, 1970

There was no talk of Mammy's bad legs
or who was minding the shop and bar
that blazing morning. *What does that signpost say?*
she'd ask with her foot on the accelerator
to a blur of lime trees and white hawthorn.
Always in a rush. Yet that day there was time
for shopping, just us, after the convent visit.
She talked about Hurleys for years afterwards
– through all our painful misunderstandings –
my red buckled Regency pumps, her navy
'wet look' slip-ons with the gold chain walking
towards us in their shop mirror and the sea
and Donavan's Hotel, plaice and tartare sauce,
our eyes on our bags and each other, riveted.

## GUARDS

*to Catríona*

For a woman full of anxieties and fear so bad
she often cried out, *When? When will it end?*
Mammy had a funny attitude to the Garda Síochána.

It was men who failed to teach her, their patience
failed them and the same kind of policers she evaded
when she sped through the back roads

of Cork, Kerry and Limerick with a provisional
licence. Laughing at our fears, laughing at the men, probing
Daddy with the accelerator although she was not shy

to look for help from any knight of the road, asking him
to park the Mini when she was too nervous or to reverse
her out of a tight spot, his corrugated brow concentrating

as she talked non-stop. I'm back in the dark
of January, she's driving me back to boarding school.
Longsuffering May is riding shotgun as I hang over Mammy

from the back seat, my arms around her, trying to clasp
the seat belt round her waist. Mammy, laughing with fear
and excitement, even as the guards are flagging us down.

The Gardaí were dreadful fairies always appearing to ask
the awkward question —out of nowhere sometimes like
that day on the Conor Pass when she was the heroine

outwitting the foxy fellow on foot in a mountain fog.
Did she give Mary's name, the sister in New York who
got the licence when they were given out without the test?

Or was it Tricia who got pressed into the impersonation
of Nuala, another red-haired sister, handing
in the licence as promised to Mallow Garda Station?

I can't be sure. I only know she got away with it, her heart
*still going*, she says, as she unclips the *suffocating* seatbelt and
releases the brakes to motor on for the Convent of Mercy,

never at rest for the whole of my life.

# LOST BUCKLE, TRAMORE AMUSEMENT PARK, 1971

Not many days out. Mass was the place for that
and everyone saying wasn't the parading desperate
as they paraded their own big hats to the altar.
The school trip to Tramore, my lilac pin-striped flares,
white polo-neck with stripes the blue-purple
of the Cadburys milk chocolate wrapper and the
enveloping synthetic taste of the 6D bar melting
on my tongue. Bumper jolts, pretending to laugh,
Roy Orbison, burnt rubber and sparks before
emerging with one naked red pump. Scrambling
every time the music stopped – which car was it?
Too shy to ask the cigarette-clamped operator,
his iron-thin legs in his faded Levis, legs of stone.

## HORSES IN THE BASEMENT
*for David*

I think of horses as I go down the steps
today. The Duhallow Hunt gathered

at Burnfort Cross in their pink coats. The Mallow
Big Shots standing in the frosty air putting the hot

toddys to their lips. How we wanted horses,
us poor relations, family of ten, envying

our cousins, one a jockey, another a show jumper.
I go down to look for Uncle Tommy –

his letter from Limerick Prison in 1921.
I want to read again the way he put his ear

to the window of his cell to hear the horse deal.
They were bringing in his dinner –

as the halter went on and the horse was led away –
new potatoes and I wouldn't mind some now

as I stand, famished, my bare feet on cold concrete
searching through boxes, standing under

the ancient fuse board, exposed wires, rusted iron
on worn wood, wondering if we have to rewire –

how will I stand the walls torn down, the horsehair
hanging out again? When I plastered the kitchen,

I wondered how Donny's ginger fur could float
so high before I realised it was old horsehair,

two hundred years old, reminding me of Ginger
in Black Beauty and how many hard-worked

sweated horses lined these walls.

They stand under John Wayne,
Henry Fonda, Warren Oates,
thin obedient ears, large eyes
pooled under soft fringes,
they whinny and trot and gallop
canter and rear
when it's called for
swim the Rio Grande, roll under
Apaches, fall with the stunt riders
off the bridge in *The Wild Bunch*,
endure pistol shots, sizzling explosives,
the prancing of Steve McQueen
in *The Magnificent Seven*,
Ben Johnson and Harry Carey Jr.
riding *alla Romana* for John Ford.
All that beauty, terror and foam –
the smell of horse sweat
and salty popcorn washed down with Coke.
They know the sound of a Winchester 73
or a Colt 45 as well as they know
the sound of their own hoof beats
and they keep galloping –
clouds of dust now across Monument Valley –
never losing their balance.

# RADIOGRAPHERS ARE THE COLDEST OF ALL

Uncle Michael said. I can't remember
if he was in Jervis Street or the Richmond.
All those Dublin Hospitals where I learned
one X-ray trade or another have gone into
the light one way or another too. It's over
thirty years since he had cancer but I still
remember the hurt and anger in his voice.
The shame I felt for a profession I hadn't
chosen myself. I'd never heard that cold
tone from him before because he was
always joking, always grámhar.
I could see her. Called in at 4 a.m.,
uniform glowing in the dim light, tan and gold
bracelets, deaf to his jokes, adjusting
kilovoltage, current and time, the steel plate
jammed down behind his back, while he sat up
perpendicular to the rays, the cross centred
on the angle of his sternum. The square
of shadow ticking on its timer. It is hard to talk
when you're doing something technical
but I had enough of the O'Shaughnessys
in me to attempt to juggle both.
I had a reputation for holding up X-ray rooms,
gassing and listening to patients' stories –
Mike Smith shouting from behind
the control panel, *Mrs Evans is still
in Room Three, writing down advice from Bridie
in the headscarf.* But I could be chill too,
numbed after ninety-five chest X-rays
in one day in the Mater chest unit
so that I dreamed all night, take a breath in,

hold it, breathe out, now turn to the left,
hands above your head. Once on a twenty-four
hour shift, I could have looked right
through the man on the table, going
into the Cat Scanner and refused
to laugh when he wondered aloud
like so many who had gone before him,
if he had any brain at all.

SKULLS

Getting the angle right meant
staring into people's eyes,
getting close, some of them
giggled. But they had to stay still
because of the radiation.
*Keep still please!* I said.
I didn't like to think of the oozing
grey matter inside. So soft
it gave me the shudders.
A baby's fontanelle made my knees
go from under me. The huge gaps
between their bones – sometimes junior
doctors took them for fractures and
scared hell out of young parents
in the middle of the night.
I'm always banging mine – in Belfast,
I ran up and down the hotel
corridor looking for 12 B.
The manager told me it was
*really number 13 –*
*But you're not suspicious surely!* he laughed.
Not superstitious in Belfast?
*Oh I am,* I said. *Please can I have 12 A?*
Which was tiny. I went in and bang!
against the angled ceiling.
I had an egg on my forehead for
the public reading. Sometimes junior
doctors followed me into the Dark
Room for my opinion but I fled
because I was sure there was nothing in
my head apart from the nineteenth century novels

I squeezed into my uniform pockets.
The Category A prisoner from Mountjoy
noted this when he sat down for his X-ray
at 4 a.m. in '87. Angling in at thirty degrees
for the Townes view, nervous
before his bleached eyes, I forgot
the lead cone left on the tube. It flew for
his head but he was faster –
catching it in his two blue tattooed hands.
*Lucky for you I caught it!* he kept saying.
*We saw nothing*! said the two prison
officers as they cuffed him again,
laughing hysterically. I watched them
walk away,
chained to each other.

# BABIES

I volunteered to do the skeletal survey
of the spina bifita foetus immediately.

The pathologist brought her in a white
bucket and I spread out the tissue paper.

I had my reasons to lay out the small
perfectly-formed rubbery doll-like

arms and legs on the X-ray table to see
if I would have the heart

to kill her again after seeing that.
When the Superintendent marveled

that a woman would put herself forward
for such a harrowing task, I wondered

when was the right time to be faint-
hearted because I remembered

his refusal when I asked for a chair
after three major bleeds, my legs

aching under me at five months,
feet burning. Encouraged

by his female deputy, he said no,
I must stand from nine to five

because there was no excuse for
laziness, *Pregnancy is not an illness.*

*In Africa, women sit down under trees
to have babies,* he said.

## NIGHTTOWN

Up all night in the Mater Hospital, pushing
an X-ray machine through fluorescent light –

I'd waited eight hours for the last coronary bypass
and when it came back, I'd given up

and gone back to bed so I had to come down
again in the old cage lift from the Doctor's Res

to the heart arrested in ITU, the body bucking,
the surgeon from Dubai shoving past me as I angled

the X-ray tube and my cross of light on the sunken
sternum. His neat brown fingers cut into

my picture. Chopping the stitches with the side
of his hand, he took out the heart and massaged

it in front of me while I heaved in my forbidden
open-toe sandals. I'd stopped wearing shoes

after my first 24 hours on call in Cork Regional.
They rang from Casualty, *RTA* –

*get up out of that quick!* the porter who knew
the whole of the Yangtze River menu by heart

shouted there were two stretchers coming up
from a road traffic accident. I sat at the side

of the narrow bed, felt for my shoes only
my feet were tender watermelons now that refused

to go in. Forcing them, I couldn't manage one
step – like an ugly sister or a step-mother,

dancing in hot iron shoes. I hoped bare feet
wouldn't be noticed in an emergency.

*And is it a gypsy you are now so?* the A&E Sister
snapped out of her blue lead apron, as I padded

around the immobilised blood & alcohol
smelling bodies with my sandbags and cassettes,

marking right and left with my metal marker,
concentrating on not mixing them up like I had

before. That bossy Sister noticed everything I did.
Next day I woke at half four, in the stuffy

on-call room, my day off already disappeared
into November darkness as I hurried

to the shoe shop in Wilton Shopping Centre.
The assistant told me that feet never stopped

growing, *Half a size for every year,*
*I'm telling you, girl* – sleepy and bewildered,

I bought a big size seven. It was only when
I revived over beans & toast at 8 o clock

that it hit me – by that reasoning I'd be size
eleven at the age of thirty, with yards

to go ahead of me. *The coffin that would hold me
hasn't been built yet!* I shouted into the empty

beige kitchen. Back in the shop next day
for an exchange – no sign of the first assistant.

The bee-hived older woman said she'd never
heard of her.

## THE MADWIFE BRINGS A FLOWER IN HER BAG

*after Pier Paulo Pasolini's Love Letters*

i forgot
from the belly
the madwife brings a flower in her bag
no the midwife comes and in her bag
she brings a flower
your uncle brought you?
the stork brought me
i was born under the blankets
i was the eachtar, the runt
there was a want in me
nobody told me
sent from god
collected at the hospital
sent down by an angel
in a lemon buttoned cardigan
a small nun all in grey
with a pale-pink baby sock hanging
off her four knitting needles
i didn't ask for it
never be ashamed
go for help
you can go away quietly
and they will arrange
for it to be adopted
jesus gives it to the stork
i know
i won't say
found crying

in a confession box
a shoe box
blue
thrown in a well
she was nursing in england
and the letter was found
she said it was fully-formed
when they took it out
the stork put it in the basket
the midwife comes
and in her bag
she carries a flower

PETHIDINE


Dr Johnson, the registrar in his scrubs
and stethoscope – middle aged and
harassed, one of those men who started late
or didn't have the luck or neck to push
for consultancy. These men were more likely
to treat us like human beings.
And Dr Johnson had pushed the stretcher
up from Casualty himself. The patient,
Mr Driscoll, smelling like a stale barrel
of porter propped up, belting out
*The Banks* in a brimming baritone, his leg
wrapped to the knee in greens.
Johnson, looking over his chart, asked me
four times if I was sure I could do
this foot. I was still young enough
to be taken as too young to be able
to take an X-ray. *I can do feet,*
*they're easy!* I shouted over
Driscoll swinging at his verse –
where we sported and played through
*each green leafy shade*. It was a lesson
in observation. Every time I saw greens
after that, I saw Johnson unwrapping
that leg on Christmas Eve,
the foot hanging off, like a door,
on its broken hinge. Driscoll,
his red mouth open,

like every other drunk on Pana,
his tongue pedalling furiously,
my hands slipping on the cassette
as he rounded to his finale, screaming out,
*For the love of Jesus – On The Banks*
*of My Own Lovely Lee.*

## CLINICAL INDICATIONS

Oh was shorthand for the chemical equation
$C_2H_5Oh$ – Ethanol meaning alcohol,
a tip-off from the doctor,
a coded message
to say drink was involved/ the patient was drunk.
The radiographer faraway
in a deserted X-ray department at night
had to watch out for the obstreperous.
It might have been shorthand for Irish
but how could *they* scare me when
I only had to lay my Cork accent
like a wand on their ears?
Once I puzzled over
a request form for a chest X-ray
that gave one word – Irish –
in the Clinical Indications box.
Was it a joke? Or working backwards,
shorthand for the drink or drunk
or look out
for the telltale fractures of the third metacarpal
from frustrated Paddies punching the wall
for the bi-lateral healed rib fractures
of the older labouring immigrants
who got so plastered they fell down,
broke, healed and carried on,
the stigmata inside the coats
of their skin like the rays from
a sacred heart? Or did it mean
what I never understood?
That night, the young doctor
with the black moustache

too close to me at 2 a.m.,
his breath in my ear, whispering –
*Something has to be done about the Irish.*
They're spreading TB, spitting it
on the floors in Kilburn.
I'm scanning another man's head
so I can't move away from
the smell of his Wotsits.
I look straight ahead while
through the microphone
on the other side of the glass
my voice echoes –
Keep still, you're doing brilliant –
to Mr MacNamara, yards away
terrified on a moving table.

## VILE JELLY

Looking at things, really looking at things
is harder, why films might be more scarring
than books except for Macbeth whose knocking
eye-words beat a tattoo in my head at sixteen.
Add to that Gloucester's vile jelly-eye extracted
and wobbling – where? In Cornwall's hand?
Or on the floor and staring up at them all as Regan
hisses, *Let him smell his way to Dover.*
Looking, looking, looking – all my life
trying to get things straight with crooked eyes
that never can line anything up.
White uniform every day for fifteen years,
shifty-eyed in my shining disguise, forced to stare
right into other people's eyes to get their sinuses straight.
That English radiographer who came down in '86 – white
– into the smoky Mater staffroom from ENT theatre
after being eyeballed by a blown-up eye on a TV monitor
during the lunch-time op. Said he'd never liked eyes.
And we were instantly and sympathetically nauseous
in our sandwiches and cigs
because we were used to orthopaedics, yellow bone
and pink muscle, electric saws and bloody swabs.
But a big eye looking at you? That was too new,
a horror – like when a bad accident came in
on the ground floor to Casualty, displaying the same
bone and muscle exposed but unexpected under
the torn denim of a leg of jeans. I had to turn
my eyes away,
cover bone and flesh with whatever I had,
X-ray through any material at all, rather than look at
what was ordinary, two floors up.

# THRONE

*Sit we upon the highest throne of the world, yet sit we upon our own tail*
– Montaigne

I feel like some kind of animal
even while I am convinced that
they are better, nobler than us –
all the usual confusions.
I am 19, standing
in the Viewing Area in Vincent's
when the tutor holds up
my first lateral lumbar spine.
As my eyes travel down each
nugget of bone to the coccyx
with its sweeping sizeable curve,
I look at her face
to see if this is some kind of freak
but her eyes are narrowed
in the usual way, I haven't got it
straight, it's too oblique
will have to be repeated
and this is bad – another 100%
dose of radiation to the gonads.

For once I'm not going through
the ground over the gonads
in this arena
where everyone scans everyone
else's mistakes, they say things like,
*Lovely pair of knees!* after you cut off
the top of a pelvis
or *He was pleased to see you!* at the giant soft tissue
erections doubly magnified because

the film-to-focus distance is so wide.
I learn the only way to stop this
is to drop a lead apron
from a height on top of them:
This is to protect your gonads.
My what?

This time the voices
of the radiologists and radiographers
have lifted into the air
as if they've moved
to another radio station –
vomit rises to my throat,
the shock of seeing
a large unmistakable tail
on an ordinary upright human
and realising in that moment
I have one too.

# MAN FALLS OFF GREENHOUSE I

There are moments at the photocopying machine
when it comes back, the panic and prickly

heat when I have to repeat again and again.
Repeats were mortal sins. 100, 200, 300% increase

in the radiation dose. Sister Patricia, grave face above
her white habit, the list of artefacts like a checking

of the conscience: remove earrings, bracelets, dentures,
toupées...And three Vincents' students asking that

man with the artificial haystack on his head, *Have
you got any jewellery, false teeth or toupées?*

Our six eyes on his head, his jaw out – *No-uh!*
before we go back behind the control panel

to turn the large knobs and peer out, puzzled
at the thatch we daren't snatch off his head.

I've had to look into the man's eyes to get it all
arm-achingly angled right, lined-up straight – the strain

has us giggling and scared by the time we arrive
in the viewing area, having slammed the three classic

skull views in their cassettes into the Darkroom hatch
AP, Lateral and Townes and waiting –

for what could we expect? We don't know, only
we are so pink and jittery, we draw Miss O'Peel's

notice down on our nineteen-year-old nervous heads.
She reaches in for the films, hangs them up

for everyone to see – a grid of lines and clips
all across the bone. *Disgusting! Unprofessional!*

The doctors look at us, disgusted too, as she
walks past us into the X-ray room and bangs as much

as one can bang a lead-lined door. We never
see what happened in there or how he parts

with his wig, the three classic skull views sail out
again on the chemical-lined river of the processor

all by themselves this time, Yorick alone
that leveller – pure luminous bone.

## A LAST LOOK AT THE GENERATOR,
## SCHOOL OF RADIOGRAPHY, ST VINCENTS', 1982

Mammy trembled before God's current
but it's man-wired electricity I fear.

The Siemens engineer took us down
to the generator at six p.m. when

even the keen were flagging.
*We'll have a last look at the generator*!

His Kildare accent thickened
with the excitement as he led

us bleary girls, dreaming of supper,
down to that back room

where he reminisced about the electricity
in his life, milliamps and resistors,

voltage gluing him to the spot,
of being *stuck to the static,*

of Herculean throws exercised
to shift heavily charged machinery,

earthing and circuits, twisted flexes,
coursing amounts of kilovoltage

*enough to kill you four times.*
I think of him every time I stand

shaking on a chair
changing a bulb.

## MAN FALLS OFF A GREENHOUSE II
*after John Donne*

That evening, newly qualified, my first time as a second on-call. The first on-call, some impressive twenty-six-year-old Senior has been coping alone. The unspoken rule is that she leaves you at home if possible but here I am at nine p.m., full of beans on toast, shaking in the IVP room before the man with Leukaemia and a glass eye. They've laid him on the Tomo Table. Tomography is the mother of Catscan, grandmother of MRI – with a big noisy swing of a heavy tube on a pole, it can take a slice of a kidney but I am trying to X-ray a skull and I only know the Skull Table, now preoccupied with a chaos of hurlers since Senior is wrestling with The Glen hurling team and many male supporters wearing raincoats clutter the waiting room as my man removes the eye. With a tear in my own eye, I touch his shoulder, begin gently. Only when I press the exposure button, the pole starts swinging because it's on Tomo and I have to repeat only now there's no penetration. It's a pale squib. So I turn up the kilovoltage not knowing that the button has reverted to Tomo and it swings again – loud, scraping, flies past his head, over and back. He's suffered enough.

He's suffered enough. I go out to apologise but he's put his eye back in so I have to ask him to take it out again – leave it, until I've checked the films. Because the socket is dry, it makes a noise I can't bear. But we go again. Only this time I fear he's moved. When I come out of the Dark Room, I bend down to collect my film to see a blur. Yes, he has moved so we have to have yet another go only he's already put the cork of his eye back in its socket, the dry sucking noise as he pulls it out again is awful although now everything is right, kilovoltage, position. Yes, Tomo button up and he's stony still only when I open the bucky tray, it's empty – I forgot the film! – and he's busy putting his very dry eye back in its hydroptic pocket. When Senior looks in on me, I'm crying, my sap sunk among the chemicals where the processor is beeping for the fixer which stinks like me, a sinful tormentor of the sick and she sits on the barrel of developer laughing, wiping her Senior eyes, *Oh leave his eye in his head, Jesus, it's hard enough. Leave everything in, they'll know what they all are when they read the films tomorrow morning. Right so. Tomo button up, open the cones WIDE, no need for pretty pictures tonight, film in the bucky. Big breath now, Mr Callaghan. Hold it!*

# BARIUM SWALLOW

What was I doing there –
the family fumbler,
the dreamy one –
where every mistake
meant another spray of radiation
and doctors lashing?
Senior radiographers
on ten feet stilts.
In at eight a.m.
in my white uniform
my wide blue belt clasped,
shaking up the chalky
strawberry-flavoured Barium
drinks before the patient was
strapped to a table and
spun fairground-style,
the radiologist watching
the image intensifier,
tracking the passage of food,
radiographers watching
the radiologist,
the cassettes and the kilovoltage.
Turning the huge Flash Gordon dials.
Dr O'Mahoney shouting,
*Drink Greedily, I said!*
The skeleton opened
its Halloween jaw and
I saw – not the opaque river
showing the faults

in the digestive system
twentieth-century style
but a medieval image
of the Time
that I was losing there
every day.

## THE AMBULANCE DRIVER SAID SHE DIDN'T LIKE MY CROCS

And I was at her mercy not wanting
to say that I'd been proud

to get my tea-towelled bloody foot
into any kind of receptacle.

They moaned from the bottom,
*Why is it always three flights!*

*Tired? Oh that's what happened to*
*the last one. He worked himself to death.*

*Literally. He was a cold – purple literally –*
*cab driver, just sixty, just now, before you.*

*Dead in his cab.* She'd be annoyed,
she said, if it was *neat and tidy* when

I unwrapped my fifty-six year old foot
implying that there was a case

for me being a malingerer,
just angling to be carried out

for my Big Night on the Homerton.
A feather-quick exam of my foot,

(later revealed to be full of glass)
and they had me on my feet.

Stumbling, following them down
my own stairs as if they'd been called out

because I'd lost my sense of direction.
This was walking on knives and my foot

didn't like it, burst its red geyser
artery at the foot of the stairs.

I was helped *then* – over the bright syrup
clotting on the front steps

and into the van where my blood pressure
was taken and me and my glass

bound tightly together for the take-off
through the streets of Hackney.

In Casualty a zombie-like fleet worked
on computers without lifting their heads

as the two of them wheeled me here
and there, looking for takers.

*Politics, politics*, she was smiling
with the proof of what they were up

against. It was past midnight when they
found a nurse station open for business.

*Those horrible Crocs,* she laughed again.
She'd had enough. She was taking a sick day

tomorrow which was *today, literally!*
*Good Idea!* I called after her from

my wheel chair, finally delivered.

## SNAKE IN MY SHOE

It starts on the train home, pins and needles
at first, a numbness spreading until my sole
is lifted, forced up inside my brown shoe.

The flat green fields after Portarlington rush past
the window. We sit facing each other across
the table – May, Mammy, Joan and myself.

I can't feel the floor. I stamp my new club
foot and Mammy gives me a look as the flat head
rears like it will go through me. First time

in Dublin. Tom and his Bank of Ireland friend
met us, there was a haze coming through the trees
in Phoenix Park, dusty lion and giraffes standing out

as if they'd been coloured in. In the dead heat of the
suffocating snake house, Tom and John banged fists
on the glass and the air around me collapsed as they

laughed, teasing. I couldn't breathe. The boa constrictor
rose like Lazarus. A pile of yellow and brown leaves
assembled into a tower of rearing muscle, throwing itself

against the glass. I couldn't stop seeing it. Even after I left
the snake house, the zoo. Even now –
in the rackety carriage, the pins and needles build

the balloon of his rage inside the small leather
enclosure of my Clarks laced-up No.1 size shoe.
He twists and swells.

AMERICAN MULES

1. *Plantar Faciitus*
   *for Owen*

   *Time wounds all heels – Groucho Marx*

Líadáin and I laughed when I found the blue
lined paper with its old scribbled note
to the convent, *Haven't I still got that desperate*
*pain in my heel!* And the worst of it is that
I've got it now. I'm the age Mammy was then.
It must be my years.
Only her pain was worse
with varicose veins and standing long nights
after ten children. I felt for her, couldn't bear,
the purple grapes clustered on her shins,
the good leg and the bad leg and when the good leg
became worse than the bad leg, it was easier
for everyone, even herself sometimes, to laugh.

2. *Pink and Red*

Brown round-toed sandals with a T-bar
and yellow wax-like plastic soles smelt of summer
in the late sixties. Once Mammy indulged me
in a light-tan thin-strapped daintier pair and I walked
up and down for her. She bought two gingham
dresses; blue and white with powder-blue ankle
socks and for the red frock, pale pink, the right
shades of pink and red could go together, she said.
Clarks shoes in a wall of grass-green boxes were

stacked up in Flynn's, the smell of the leather,
the ladder, the cool steel measuring machine when
I extended my pink stockinged foot like Jesus, the
long foxy hair of the assistant spilled over my feet.


*3. Saturday Night and Sunday Morning*

Saturday nights were something then before
Nuala got married so I must have been less than
four – the shoes laid out, polished the night before.
Nuala's work with help from the younger ones,
shining shoes, lined up, empty of feet like
our stomachs empty of food, the acrid scent
of Kiwi polish intensified by our fast.
The high expectation of the ironed dresses laid out
with socks and cardigans, Nuala's suspenders and
stockings – it was before tights.
On Sunday we ran down the road after Mass
to open the shop and bar, before a dressed-up crowd
pursuing us for Powers, Guinness, and Cadburys.

## 4. Are You Ready, Boots?

But who took us shopping? Who
decided in '72 that we would be
encased in high fashion?
Tricia, Ber and me aged eighteen, fourteen,
and eleven, always in a row in photos.
Tricia had the smallest foot, gloved in yellow
tan with a Pompadour heel, buttoned up
to mid-calf. Ber's platforms – dark as the shell
of a Choc Ice – ended mid-patella.
Mine were laced, criss-cross
knee high, white leather (plastic probably).
Tom examined and pronounced mine
the best, if only, he qualified, I could put
my two mauve legs into the one boot.


## 5. We're Off to See the Wizard

Photos from the seventies and Ber
looks tall and leggy in denims
that flare to the ground, curtaining
her platforms. She took a six-inch ruler
to the shoe-shop and jeans had to be
carefully hemmed over those rocking
cliff wedges. I knelt at her feet
with the pins in front of the mirror.
When drainpipes came in, she had to
step down and become small like
the Wizard of Oz.

## 6. Hard on Shoes

Mammy examined my run-down heels, said
I was hard on shoes and it was true, I threw
myself hard into everything. My Biro indented
the page. My eraser rubbed holes in my copybook,
the page lit up by the Master's absinthe eye
staring through at me before he ran for the stick.
My books too – squeezed, flattened, pawed with butter,
dripped with cocoa, pushed into pockets and once
between the covers of a missal when I hoped to get away
with reading Enid Blyton in Mass. *Animal Farm*
left after the picnic at the Mass Rock, drenched
by rain, ruffled by the wind, swollen like my feet
inside the oven of the kitchen range in Burnfort.
I didn't notice my shoes burning, turning the pages.


## 7. Holy Ground

I avert my eyes passing shoeshops but
the devil peers out, ruby eyes illuminating
a window in Venice, filled with expensive
colours of chocolate, donkey, desert.
Mary Magdalene unbuckling Jesus's dusty
lachets, all those people in the Bible
showing off their toes, the gleaming Mary-Janes
Líadáin begged for at six, strapped
to her feet by the assistant in Clarks –
a communion so intense she was still
whispering outside the shop, picking
her way along the pavement
on Holloway Road. She was afraid, she said
they might speak to her.

*8. You Can't Go Out Like That*

*For Katie*

It took Líadáin a long time to forgive me
for saying those yellow-tongued pumps were
like something a prostitute would wear.
Later I bought MBTs for plantar fasciitus,
convinced by the testimonials claiming
foot cures as powerful as the touch
of a saint's bone – and just as attractive.
Liane said they were supposed to give you
a tight butt but I wanted comfort. Wrapped
in fake fur, ear muffs, blue cross and chain,
I rocked by the hall door on my giant
trainers and Líadáin said, *You can't go out*
*like that, Mum,* you look *like a rapper!*


*9. American Mules*

*For Lucy McDiarmid*

I never painted my nails or wore high heels.
I was not proud of my rough hands and

stubby toes. I winced to see the ugly sisters
hurting themselves. I would even go a step

further and say I always identified
with donkeys. Líadáin at nine agreed:

with your patient brown eyes and hardworking ways.
But when Mary opened her American suitcase

with the scent of Estée Lauder's Youth Dew
real leather and Hershey bars, shook out

the white dress patterned with red and blue boats
held by a wide red sash, it was made

for me. I zipped in as she held out scarlet
high-heeled mules to match.

Why shouldn't you wear them? Go on,
slide your foot inside. It was easy

going to Dublin from Mallow – a train carriage
the safe place for high heels, never far

from a hand clutch in a narrow space
where everyone staggered but never fell.

It was only when I clicked out onto the black
and white tiles of Heuston that I was

checked – even half a polished square
was too much without a handhold.

The people shoved past with their callous
handbags as I trembled on the shining floor

half-leaning against the sunlit dusty orange
and black carriage, inching forward and back

swaying for what must been a minute but
felt like an hour before I gave in, stepped down

trotted barefoot to the taxi rank,
the red mules hanging from my hands.

# X-RAYING FEET

*For Maureen*

When we were students at Vincent's, the tutor
never touched feet, her oval red nails checked
the yellow request form, then dropped it back
in the polished wooden box. A present
for someone else and feet were good practice
for students anyway. Positioning not difficult –
just place the steel plate under the naked feet,
centre the cross in the rectangle of ticking light.
Only we didn't like touching feet either
and we never knew when opening laces and buckles and zips
would release a bomb or some bad surprise
like the workman from Ballinamona
who only washed the affected foot:
*God, are ye going to do the both of them?*
sitting embarrassed with a black foot and
a white foot on the cassette.
Even the clean ones left moist anxious prints on the metal.
Patients were just as relieved as radiographers –
down in the underground hum of the Mater Casualty –
in the blood-soaked alcoholic shrieking
average one hundred patients for one person to X-ray in one night –
when feet were X-rayed through socks and desert boots.
*What are these?* the radiologist might point
to the metal eyeholes of a boot projected across the phalanges
or metatarsals or the shadow of a rubber sole
on a film the following morning
knowing already he was too late
the yawning 24-hour radiographer responsible
was dreaming at home, the limping patient
long gone down Eccles Street
or the North Circular Road.

## FOURTEENTH HEARING AT THE ROYAL COURTS OF JUSTICE

*The couple sued Hello! for £2m for stress, loss of income and damage to their professional careers because of the poor quality of the photos...Hello! published several snatched shots of the wedding reception including one photograph of Ms Zeta Jones eating wedding cake...Ms Zeta Jones, 33, said she felt 'violated' when Hello! published the unauthorised photographs, which she claimed were 'sleazy and unflattering'.*
*The Guardian,* 11 April 2003

*The Royal Courts of Justice (London's High Court) is an enchanting building on London's Fleet Street.*
theroyalcourtsofjustice.com

Down Chancery Lane, past Ravenscroft's window, makers of legal wigs for centuries – Humphrey Ravenscroft patented the horse-hair wig in 1834, cheaper than human hair and more practical – and onto The Strand, through the enchanting gates and arches of the Royal Courts, past the stone cat and dog representing fighting litigants, the figures of the Saviour, Alfred, Moses and Solomon who suggested that a child should be cut in half.

We pass the Costume Museum, wait with counsel at the oak tables in The Bear Gardens. The judge is a woman skilled in family matters, a child's peace of mind in her balance. The morning passes but she never appears. We leave, tired, some thousands lighter, to wait another six months. Paparazzi position their cameras at the railings. Tomorrow Michael Douglas and Catherine Zeta Jones will successfully sue *Hello! Magazine.*

## WATCH

The night before my wedding
I put my wristwatch through the machine cycle.
It was not in a jeans pocket or tied to a belt,
not wrapped in a T-shirt
nor balled up in a pair of tights.
No. I put it in the empty machine,
shut the door and turned
the wheel of the switch revving the Bosch
to life. Standing nonplussed on the concrete floor
of the bottle shed, it dripped in my hand
after the 40 minute cycle.
I'd been wondering what
was inside and then I remembered
like I was watching someone else
bending to place the watch inside the drum
carefully, like a bundle of delicates
turning the dial like a sleep-walker.
I could hear the clink of glasses
and murmur from the bar as
I went out into the dark and stars
of the backyard to take
the futile action of hanging
the glittering face by its worn strap
from the clothesline
up to my ankles
in wet grass.

# THE CLERK AT THE FAMILY COURT

*Don't you find it all very expensive?*
He leans across the desk.
Dark-skinned, tall, narrow-faced,
on dark days he looks most handsome.
He's got a gold tooth.

His is the first human face I see
after the security men
the X-raying of my bag
and bundles of documents.

The Tannoy strikes
through the building.
*Would all parties in the case of Evans*
*please make their way to court No. 15*
*on the third floor.*

Once he let Líadáin sit
in the judge's seat after a session.
That was the fairest thing
that happened to her at court.

He keeps an eye out
at the entrance
when I'm too sick to look myself,
flashing his gold tooth at me
every other month this year,
the third year of it,
when our Catherine Wheel floats round
to his desk
and he leans over,
*don't you find all this very expensive?*

## MY PERSEPHONE

Was it the small red crab apples crushed flat
making the Holloway pavements flush
with their trees' harvest, the brown leaves

on the ground, the bombed conkers,
the fact I was ten days late
that made me think she was Persephone?

I already knew her sex, despite my best intentions,
the temptation of working in X-ray – I'd spread the gel,
scanned the shadowy form, turning prettily.

Now it was 3pm on the day. I'd been in labour since 2am
but he'd wanted to have lunch with his cousin (and drinks)
Go, I said. Who wants a man who wants to be elsewhere?

I made a Mr Guinness cake which wouldn't bake
in the centre, hopping around the yellow kitchen
with the skewer, as the cramps tested me.

I packed a suitcase full of books and pens and papers
I rang my sister about the vomiting.
Could it be a stomach bug? she wondered.

I rang the Whittington, they weren't taking us
serious either. You've plenty time, Sister Murphy said an hour
before she said I was too dilated, too late for the epidural

I'd been persuaded was a must for a nervous person
like myself who was writing a poem about Persephone
during the second stages of labour and Pluto was –

where else? – down below in the pub.

## EVERYTHING INCLUDING THIS ROOM
## IS A FUTURE RUIN

And when the wind is finished
with us, the rain starts.
I think it will never

stop – worried
by cracks in the wall and
the lump of dislodged lead

that is directing
the rain down into the brick
so that a tobacco-coloured

liquid drips down
the inside of the window
and some strange yellow

cauliflowers are growing
inside the kitchen walls.
In 1999 I slept high

in the bird's nest.
Marcel and Alice were
kittens and the night after

I took up the fragmenting
1970s carpets, their paws
thundered on the floorboards

frightening me. Now
2014, I've gone to ground
like a badger in the basement

to be close to the garden,
and the sounds
have changed as the cats jump

from table to floor over
my head and pass in and
out the flap a dozen times.

Donny growls low
in his ginger belly
and I see the fox

so close, his brown-fawn
face like a friend's
and it is hard

to see him run from us,
his bare rump –
something's made his fur fall

out, he runs up the spiral
staircase, I run to the backdoor.
I want to welcome him

but he is on the fence,
then Martin's galvanized roof
and gone.

## MRS SCHIFF'S WASHING MACHINE

*I wanted to tell you that just by looking at the pictures in the
ad again, after I have seen the space, a very warm feeling filled
my soul, myself living in there is such a joyful feeling to be
having. Also you should know that I am a non-smoker and very
respectable when it comes to the space I live, to me it's like the
temple of my life really.*

It was Socrates who broke the door
of the machine like he broke many
things, the smell of his Moroccan Gold
rising through the inch-wide cracks
in the floorboards, lemon bars filling
with light every evening. Hell
can be funny from a distance
and sometimes up close
like the night we were watching
Michael Cacoyannis's *Iphigenia* –
drums and bloodthirsty chants
pressing Agamemnon to his agonised
decision. *Those infernal drums!* he shouts
as Socrates, on cue, sends up thunder
from his toubeleki through the smoke
and someone sings,
*Spare me the frenzy of passion!*
I had to tell him to go in the end.
He was not a bad man – it was just that it was
like being married again.
*And he broke the door of Mrs Schiff's washing machine,*
I just couldn't get over it.
Scrubbing and throwing out many smoke-ruined things,
*He didn't even have the gumption to tell me!*
Failed landlady, I didn't have the gumption

to keep some of his deposit.
After he left, I gathered back Mrs Schiff's
unbroken everyday plates – 1970s elegance,
cream stoneware with green rims
& idealised peaches.
When we lay them on the table now
it's the nearest thing we have
to saying Grace – here in the Temple
of my Life. Really.

on the phone, red cyclamens against
the desert-brown twigs of the garden, waiting
to talk to Virgin Media, Three, Petplan Insurance,
the wind howls in the pipe of the copper stove
like Masha said it did before Father's death
in Chekhov's *Three Sisters*. Three say the mobile's
still not free on a 0800 number
and the landline cuts out four times
while talking to the Arts Council
when it is revealed that no one including
myself knows the right name for the application –
am I Evans for writing or Cotter for
the Bank which is, of course, low in funds
or Cotter in England for the National Insurance
or Evans in Ireland for the PPSN?
I was at a wedding in Killorglin
when a woman told me that
I was really Mrs. Knightly-Evans –
*They dropped the Knightly after the Freestate*
she said, *because it was bad for business.*
*And all the Mrs Knightly-Evans's die violent deaths.*
My hand on the phone grows stiff and suddenly
it is evening,
the crumbling old window Dickens-black with dust.
Donny has a rash and he's only just come off the insulin.
He doesn't like the Grannick's Bitter Apples
I sprayed to stop him licking. He runs out the catflap.
and I run after him, wishing I could be hands-free.
*I'm sorry, I'm sorry,* I am calling, nearly weeping
as he leads me to our summer hide-out
under the pergola and the phone breaks down

again and I throw it into the grey sticky London
clay-earth I was digging this morning.
Donny stands over my head on the roof
of hydrangea branches like a monument
in his kerchief and we stay there in the dark
for a long time together listening to
the wind in the leaves.

## SECRETS AREN'T ALWAYS SURPRISES

I put on my red coat, took my purse.
I was a woman staying with her in-laws
in County Kerry. I didn't even

like the television squatting
in the centre of that house but when
I raised my eyes from my book,

saw the ad for a *velvety* new chocolate
bar – that purple-navy packet
became my urgent secret quest.

Speeding up through the hawthorn
corridor of the side road, I burst
onto the main road with

its boulders weightily parked and
placed to bar the Travellers' caravans.
Heavy passing trucks reminded

me of Mammy crying out, *Throw
yourself into the ditch before they
suck you under their wheels!*

In the shop the girl stared.
I remembered being the girl in the
shop. Hiding my book under

the counter, surreptitiously chewing
a Pineapple Split. Quietly unwrapping
the purple-navy Aztec wrapper.

I was the girl in the shop
and the woman who'd broken out –
or was it in? – for a chocolate bar.

The woman who said, *I'd like
a Surprise, please!* might be wild-eyed.
*I'd like a Surprise, please,*

I repeated my menacing request
as she backed away. The smell
of oranges, Sour Cherry bubble-gum,

the vanilla of biscuits. Her
face clearing – *Oh you mean
the Cadbury's Secret.*

## THROUGH THE GLASS

*For Eileen*

Auntie Helen had a Spar shop too
but it smelt sweeter than ours,
the wood-effect Lino softer
like toffee, under my tan sandals.
And when she brought us out of
her diminutive sitting room –
where I sat looking at the yellow teapot
in the shape of a house, the fluorescent
strip of light fluttered and sang.
Mars and Milky Way, forbidden
and stolen at home, tasted different here.
I listened to the flat County Limerick accents,
mentally spending my first wage packet –
first thing on the list, a teapot in the shape of
a house. Auntie Helen told the sharpest
stories. The sisters were always in tears
saying goodbye, black night outside
the shop window with its red letters –
It's cheaper by far to shop at Spar! –
rain on the road to Charleville,
a white paper of bag of far better
sweets on my lap, going home to Cork.

# OYSTERS

*'One on 'em,' reported Sam to Mr Pickwick, 'one on 'em's got his legs
on the table, and is a drinking brandyneat; while t'other one, him in
the barnacles, 'as got a barrel o' Oysters atween his knees, vich he's a
openin' like steam, and as fast as he eats 'em he takes a aim vith the
shells at young dropsy (the fatboy) who's, a sittin' down fast asleep in
the chimbley corner.'*
– Charles Dickens, *Pickwick Papers*


It feels good everyone says so
warm and small like a doll's
house and because it never housed
anyone with the money to exercise change
all the fireplaces intact
and the eight-paned internal window
of the basement bedroom
looking into the low hallway,
(although the concrete floor must
have been mud before) and
the garden earth full of artefacts –
pram wheels, green glass china milk
bottle tops, monstrously thick
broken crockery
and seam after seam of oyster shells
because that's what they ate,
washed down with stout
the pastrycook assistants,
butcher boys and nursemaids who
lived in these poor rooms
with their grand pretensions,
all decked out in miniature
the piano nobile windows
on the first floor, the laughably

appropriate architraving
for servants and their betters
and yet at night when
I hear noises and the cats stare
when the picture of Our Lady
of Guadalupe is transported
by the optical illusion of the Camden Passage
lamp and the eight panes of glass
to hover over the narrow basement stairs
despite all my childhood fantasies
of time travel and poking Henry, the Eighth
in his fat sectarian brocade
with my future finger,
I am afraid I'll see them:
so small and sickly, pre-
penicillin – and the smell.
I imagine them like the Irish fairies,
low-sized, half-human, strange-looking.
I've never liked oysters
on the table either –
rough and slithery
dirty-looking and capable
of killing you –
like some awful 19th Century disease
like general paralysis of the insane,
like syphilis.

# THE IRISH AIRMAN PARACHUTES TO EARTH

*For wisdom is the property of the dead,*
*A something incompatible with life; and power,*
*Like everything that has the stain of blood,*
*A property of the living...*
– 'Blood and the Moon', W.B. Yeats

I know that I shall meet my fate
somewhere near the ground.
Perhaps the basement where
I sleep now. I can't see
the moon there except in June
when it rides so low, I put
my two rough gardening hands
on the window frame, peering
out to the left where it appears
between two buildings and I can't
decide if it's flashing a signal
or trying to hide.
The cats circle me, *in courtly fashion*
leaping in and out through
the green curtains onto the sill,
specially softened for them
with pink and grey Mexican blankets.
Their pupils fill with black to allow
more light while the roses glow white
over the crepuscular giant shadows
of the castor oil plant.
I don't think the cats look at the moon.
I think they just happen to glance
in that general direction.
All they want is to be told –
like my father told his cats

with his rough hand,
the light touch of his crooked fingers on their fur –
that they are not alone,
that they are important,
as for being wise,
it's hard to be sure.
Even cats are surprised into falling,
fooled by shadows
blindsided.

## UNICORNS
*For Liane*

Jorge Luis Borges

It's a great comfort to know that we can't
know them and so the two I have outside
in the garden can rest assured I won't tell
anyone although I'm telling you now and
they have many disguises, bleached white
in a hot May, coy behind the bluebells
they are pretending to be white horses with one spike each
where the plaster fell off their left ears – how did
that happen? The exact same thing to each one?
That's no coincidence. In the rain
their peeled patches darken and they become
piebalds or palaminos. Broken and thrown
out of a grand house in Hampstead
to lie in the salvage yard next to Mr Allsorts'
shop and we'd just come to a turn
after a stack of butler sinks and an old toilet
painted with lotuses when Líadáin cried out and
I was sure she was right – *look, two unicorns!*
I didn't have the price of a bus fare that day
but I asked the man to put them away for us.

## WUTHERING HEIGHTS
*For Kraige*

It's never far away from me despite
being no longer young or romantic
and when Dora runs free across the pergola
she reminds me more of Kate Bush
than a Norwegian Forest Cat.
It was the darkness
that captured me years ago:
Lockwood in his oaken Georgian bed
the sliding panels like a coffin.
Cathy calling outside,
the cruelty of her arm sawn across the glass.
Even in my dreams last night when Líadáin
came down to the basement
frantic to tell me that someone was
calling and knocking in the back garden
outside my casement window
and even in my stark terror when I lifted
my head from under the covers
in the lightening room –
which I could see was empty now
except for Dora's shaggy silhouette –
I couldn't help asking the dream-Líadáin
even though I knew the real Líadáin
was still asleep in her own room,
*Was it like Wuthering Heights?*

## LONDON

Feverishly, I return, always running
from Ireland and built-up
yellow brick calms me
like green fields for others.
And over Waterloo Bridge I go
holding on to my hat in the wind,
lights strung out on the water
the babble on the 76 of 77 languages,
trundling to Dalston where the Turks
are polishing their pomegranates
and Joey and myself yap through
the basement window over our mugs
of Blackstrap Molasses.
This afternoon standing
in the biting cold at Mile End
the familiar electronic drone
announcing *277 to Highbury Corner*,
quickened me as if I'd come to a turn
in the black night, saw in a blaze
the lights of home.

## TRIGEMINAL NEURALGIA

I tell her that an early night makes all the difference to the pain.
I try to get to bed by ten, but it's now quarter to one
and she's still on the couch,
looking at me, wrapped in my woolen hat
with her metaphorical chin in her metaphorical hand.
She's wondering if it's Líadáin leaving the nest
that's caused it or perhaps it's the pressure
of having memorised my own poems.
Her forefingers chop out
a chunk in the air
to show me there's only room for so much.
I touch my hand to my woollen brow –
feel a poem coming on.

# THE CATS OF BALL POND ROAD

*1. Shakespeare Knew Cats*

> *What, drawn, and talk of peace! I hate the word*
> *as I hate hell, all Montagues, and thee!*

He is not complimentary, no doting Facebook snapper,
a man of his time when it comes to the despised feline.
One weird sister has Greymalkin and Bendedick,
*Hang me in a bottle like a cat and shoot me* while Tybalt
is the *Prince of Cats.* If we hadn't named the usurping
Burmese from De Beauvoir Road, The Viper
because of his threatening neck moves,
he would be Tybalt. *Do you bite your thumb at me sir?*
*no, I do not bite my thumb at you, sir but I bite my thumb, sir.*
*You lie!* Off it kicks as Donny-Romeo leaps in defence –
I run below the high fence imploring like Benvolio
*part fools, put up your swords you know not what you do!*
to all I can see of Donny-Romeo, his tail bloated with rage,
deaf to me, roaring, *it fits when such a villain is a guest.*
*I'll not endure him.* The ladies on the balcony,
Dora and Alice get on their hind legs to watch the show
the gold and green of their eyes vanishing into dark
pupils *burning like coals* as the toms crash along
the honeysuckled pergola, giant eyes fixed on one another.
*This stupidity will come back to bite you,* Donny-Romeo.
Fang to fang is no *holy palmer's kiss* – it is life and death
when teeth carry poison that but one month ago made
your ginger cheek round as an orange. AIDS
and feline flu' are passed freely over these garden walls
and The Viper-Tybalt is impervious to the water weapon.
Hose and rattling steel bucketfuls have I thrown over him
while he stands his dripping ground like *a princox, a saucy boy*

*wilful choler* makes him shake and I am as helpless
as before my own wilful self. This, like everything human,
will be played out on the hormones, I won't be given a say
until I'm nursing Donny-Romeo, dealing with *the bitterest gall*
the veterinary bill, broken bones.


## 2. Lying in bed in Balls Pond Road with Dora

The wind's travelling forty-five miles per hour
wisteria blossoms fall and flood
into every corner of the house.
I shouldn't leave the casement window open
after what happened to the bathroom window in 2013 –
but I have to smell the lilac before it passes on.
The children are screaming from De Beauvoir
School playground like they're being turned
on the spit of a rollercoaster.
Dora jumps on the windowsill,
her beard streaming like Jeremiah the prophet.
The wind lifts its fist every few minutes,
pillaging the Fuchsia Riccartonii,
throwing the terracotta pots around.
I would go out to save my Cheyenne Spirit Echinacea
if I wasn't trying to write this poem.

## 3. The Engine Running

*Soft Morning City! Lsp! I Am Leafy Speafing*
*in the twingling of an eye…*
– James Joyce, *Finnegans Wake*

I heard a song
and when I peered out, I knew it was
eight o clock because
the light had entered the old porch through
the cracked glass in the six-inch window.
The man on his steering wheel
filmed Donny on his iPhone
when we went out on the front step,
the grey tent of sky sagging with rain
a seagull screaming on its rope
of air, an ambulance
and a fire engine, all screaming
while the traffic rumbled on –
a low earthquake of cars
and omnibuses for more than a hundred years
and horses here in Hackney before that.
Will it ever stop and flood
like that dream
when I opened the front door
and there was nothing
but a canal
flowing down
the Balls Pond Road
like it was Amsterdam
and someone said:
*the book of depth is closed*
*step out of your shell.*

## 4. Invisible Birds

*The new knowledge the human race is acquiring does not compensate
for the knowledge spread only by direct oral transmission, which, once
lost, cannot be regained or transmitted: no book can teach what can be
learned only in childhood...*
– 'The Blackbird's Whistle', *Mr Palomar*, Italo Calvino

Marcel takes long steps
in response to the Songs
of Garden Birds, his voice frozen
mid-meow as he investigates
under the bed.
*I think it's coming from down here,*
he seems to be saying over his shoulder
before he goes under the quilt
and then as always, I press stop
not wanting to confuse or upset them,
remembering Alice's rigid belly
creep after the barn owl sounded
his hollow note on track 20.
In 70's Burnfort, the flat-capped
men in the bar asked each other
if anyone had heard the corncrake yet,
their Nostradamus heads nodding
over mounds of cut tobacco
behind bushes of Condor smoke
their questioning so intent that
the quickened note of their voices
summoned me from my book,
my bored young head
inside in its thick plate glass
sitting up for once to listen.

*5. Love*

I couldn't help it.
I gathered cats and dogs to my chest
*I love you, I love you,* I said,
squeezing them hard
even though I knew they didn't like it.
I wanted to be gentle like Daddy – dogs' eyes swam
when he placed his crooked swollen hands on their hairy brows.
*I'm back, I'm back!* he shouted
as his seventeen cats poured in an unbroken pilgrimage
down the fragmented path to greet him
after any absence. They quivered
at the sound of his flat County Limerick accent,
nuzzled into what he called their vessels,
old tin lids piled up with chunks of ham, corned beef
chicken and ham roll stolen from the shop.
Feed all the birds – that was his policy.
He tossed pieces of Keating's fresh pan into the air.
Sparrow, blackbird, jackdaw, crow or pigeon,
not one bird was classified as vermin –
only the flies were a different kettle of fish.
Eschewing spray,
he favoured the quiet stickiness of fly paper:
twelve amber strips hung,
streaming from the low wood ceiling of the shop
and he moved among them like a gardener,
hissing gently.

*6. The Death of Eileen Murphy from Cancer of the Mouth, 2004*

the vet pried her mouth open
glossy streamers of blood gushed over the white tissue
he shook his head
i threw myself across the stretcher as if she was in the line of fire.
he agreed to do it at home
she ran the blood still pouring
a magician's scarf pulled out of her mouth
i lit a fire sprinkling sugar on the coals
because she was always twice her size grinning
in the glow of pink, white and mallow-coloured flames
the vet came in from the cold
his coat rattled and he smelt of cigarettes
he said it is time
he said it is time
his coat rattled and he smelt of cigarettes
when he came in from the cold
she was always twice her size grinning
in the glow of pink, white and mallow-coloured flames
i lit a fire sprinkling sugar on the coals
a magician's scarf pulled out of her mouth
as she ran, the blood still pouring
he agreed to do it at home
as if she was in the line of fire I threw myself across the stretcher
he shook his head
glossy streamers of blood gushed over the white tissue
the vet pried her mouth open

*7. Life Calls For Death*

I take my broom
to the lost wisteria blossoms
that rained down in yesterday's
fast wind like snow.

Donny crunches a ladybird
when we sit in the sun.
I shudder thinking about it
as I open his can of John West.

The wren calls and a blackbird
sings, the cats stare up
making kk kk noises.

Later Donny is at the end
of the path,
feathers flutter down from
his mouth like black snow.

*8. Time Management*

*For Julia*

The Dalston night is still warm,
the jasmine strong. I'm wondering,
as I lock up, if these rotting windows
could keep anyone out. Even the wisteria
gets in and snakes dizzily around
the kitchen wall in September.

A musical groan from the balcony tells me
the night is not over for Donny
ensconced on the comfy orange corduroy
chair – it was for us but it's his now,
his striped marmalade coat and imposing figure
blending with the saffron cord.

He croons again to me – so
I stay a while but he knows
I'm itching to go. He stands up on
the garden table and figure-of eights
with the fairy lights – anything to stop me
deserting like a Gethsemane apostle.

My back aches and I want to finish
Season Three of *The Leftovers* so I can
work very hard tomorrow. I pluck
some leaves of catnip for him
before I go, his unsatisfied longing
a weight as I climb the stairs

to the bedroom where Dora
the Norwegian Forest Cat
sits beside the TV, waiting
her turn. She wants the special massage
I learned from a YouTube video
made by a confident man with a shaved head,
*Learn Reiki in just five minutes!*

## AS STUPID AS A TENOR

People would say, *Is there something wrong*
*with my shoulder?* because that was where
my eyes would alight – and they might
as well have been a pair of birds
for all the control I had over them.
But I enjoyed having a good look
at the man in the Green Inks bookshop –
he didn't look anyone
in the eye either so I was able
to study the effect as he glared off
to the side. He went to a lot of rounds
to get commemorative stamps
because he couldn't bear
the sight of the Queen's head.
Adult Ed teacher training 2005 –
the clown wouldn't stop picking on me.
In one of those small groups
he pointed two fingers into his own eyes,
*Focus, focus, look me in the eye, come on!*
In another small group, two posh actors
declaimed, *No such thing as class any more!*
The psychologist explained how fuck buddies
worked, no one could agree on the best
way to deal with a student who stank and
I only felt safe with the woman
who taught Kung Fu to Music.
When the jazz singer said, *One has to be intelligent*
*to sing*, the man who did something
with string quartets said, *But*
*doesn't anyone remember that saying*
*down at the Royal Opera House –*
*as stupid as a tenor?*

## THE SWITCH
*after Seán Ó Ríordáin*

*Ta eirim aigne ar an cailín sin,* that girl has ability
of the mind, Stanley would say in Irish class
as I sat with my Physics book open on the desk.

I thought I was reaching for a different plane
but now when I read O'Ríordáin's poem
where the man Turnbull changes places

with the horse – *Turnbull's* eyes *starting out from
that suffering horse's pelt* are somehow
Stanley's eyes: the colour of Bass beer

under the big triangle of light-brown curly hair
which sprang out like Athena from his head –
refusing to stay down to one side.

He didn't hide the white wart remover
painted once on his knuckles
and was nearly always patient for the five years

I wasted in his class after Monty beat
the devil into me in Burnfort National School
with a few scraps of the hated language.

These days I puzzle on my own
over O'Ríordáin and Dineen
*os a chionn sa london* – over in London.

Physics sees Time as a fundamental arrow,
there's no way back, only patchy memories.
I make my living from teaching poetry now

stand like Stanley, all my warts on show.

# READING SEÁN Ó'FÁOLAIN TO THE ENGLISH
# IN THE YEAR 2001

*There, on the old battered sofa, lay my father his head bandaged round
and round, his right hand wrapped in layers of cotton.*

I leave London for Berkshire from Waterloo, reading
Seán Ó'Fáolain on his R.I.C. father, injured during an eviction.
I don't even know what 'teaching autobiography' means – five

women and one man from sixty to ninety, polished oval table,
deep-sink carpet in the board-room, tea tray, fruit cake,
words dropping on the page like apples in autumn.

*A Place called Watergrasshill…where he'd joined a squad
of police forcibly evicting…*

But other memories run through their white heads, bring me
to an unknown place of evacuations, bitter separations, bombs &
wardens. World War Two never meant England for me.

It was Anne Frank, Poland or Germany. Churchill was a fat cigared
caricature in Burnfort, the war remembered as a shortage of
tea, Tomeen's triumphant bicycle ride with two pounds of it.

*…iron bar through a hole in the window… looked black, but it had come,
one minute before, red-hot from the hearth…seared his hand to the bone.*

War stories spark, lights coming on one after another, faces
shining in the mandorla of the table, 'I climbed all over Dad
in his fireman's uniform. I didn't want to let go of him…'

'She took us down into the sea, five evacuees up to our waists in salt
water. She called to God.' No bananas and air raids and bananas again.

'My mother in tears with two brown paper bags.' 'Starved.

Guinness and cheddar in the parlour in front of us, 'Should we
give the evacuees some cheese?' 'No, it will give them bad dreams.'
June still steals cheese, hand mousing a Sainsbury bag on the No. 8 bus.

I read them Seán Ó'Fáolain: *How fair it was you were the foolah to catch
the blow and snatch the bar…Oh the blackguards to do that to a quiet man…*

Bored and uncomfortable, they don't know what I am on about but
one remembers making her own gym knickers, 'post-war austerity'.
Then they all remember, 'Oh! That horrid crotch!'

A mother & daughter, side by side, write identical apart from
Mother recalling The Great War , 'One uncle came
to the nursery to say goodbye. I remember his enormous shoes.'

Coal: the pink, blue, lilac flames in the nursery fire, 'I could
stare for hours!' 'Not much fun for the maid dragging it up,'
says someone else. 'Oh! I never bothered about that!'

On the train back, O'Faolain again. My Nationalist orphan
grandmother opposed that armed constabulary, fighting in the
Land War but how can I ever tell them about her sojourn

in Limerick Prison in 1889 when they don't even understand
the R.I.C.? *Men like my father were dragged out, in those years.*
Granny Cowhey was supposed to be 'a lady', refused to drink

from a tin mug, insisting on a china cup & saucer, they said.
In Kilmainham, I saw Anne Devlin's small quarters, Emmet
and Parnell's spacious gentleman chamber.

Had they time in Limerick Prison to be ferrying china cups to a
twenty-three year old country girl even if she was a big tenant
farmer? Who was with her? No female political prisoners in 1889.

*And shot like traitors to their country*

The train flies through the green Home Counties. I bend
my head again to my book, *Shot for cruel necessity – so be it.*
Shot to inspire necessary terror – so be it.

June's hand moves for the cheese inside the Sainsbury bag.

But they were not traitors.

## SEVENTY-SEVEN

*We look at the world once in childhood.*
*The rest is memory.*
– Louise Glück

So who was wrong and who started it?
The old men from my childhood appear.
No one stands round shouting, *Fight! Fight!*
that's for sure, only throwing themselves in
like sandbags to stop other men from hurting
each other. In that bitter smell of porter round
the bar, a man sprawls on the red, white
and blue tiles, his flat cap tossed beside him
on the floor. He looks up bewildered.
What happened? What came over him like the wind?
The awful wail before the anguish is pressed down
again. Everyone saying it is all right now.

Fists up. Tom Twomey with his lower lip
out under his pipe refusing to give his name
in English to the Guards. *Tomás Ó Tuama*
*Ráth an Toiteáin*, he repeats, his face as mauve
as a mallow. Michael comes home with
the alternative version of the Civil War:
How come you never told us about Dirty Dick
and the seventy-seven hanged Republicans, ha?
A minute before, Tom and Daddy toasting
their caps in front of the fire for Fifi the toy
Yorkie to curl up in – now they have Michael up
against the wall, the two of them breathless,
false teeth chattering, shouting, *Bad Breeding*!

Peter comes down the stairs in a vest and
trim '70s underpants with the blunderbuss
under his arm – something else that appeared
and disappeared in Burnfort for no reason
I could see, like Jock the Shetland, stationed
in the field for one year. He seemed to love me
but always ran for the nettles and threw me there.
Daddy, a cross animal himself, inarticulate rage coursing
through his small bullock body sparked by the key
words; *De Valera, seventy-seven, Dirty Dick.*
Mammy crying, *You've upset the girls! I'll send
for the priest,* his sons never sure what side
they're on – Peter, always feeling
responsible, trying to do something about it.

Returned Yanks

All that family are tall with prominent
cheekbones. Even I can see that they
must have been good-looking once – now
they are wrinkled as twice-used tin foil.

They know New York, mention places
like The Bronx, Washington Heights as if
those streets run outside the bar door,
are spread out behind O'Sullivan's ditch.

Sweaters, pencil skirts, turned-up trousers
from the forties, fifties, they smoke sixty
a day and adore each other, howling
at the fresh grave of each sibling.

*Look at that for nature,* Mammy says,
suspecting we won't howl for her.
The brothers buy Brylcreem in the shop,
their hair partings knife-white straight

as Gable or Bogart. They must have been
handsome once but they look like Count
Dracula now. They all drink, call for
*Highballs* with a twang. They speak of

*pocketbooks*. Are always dying. Always
sitting in Mammy's upstairs sitting-room
for the Chief Mourners. Funerals are huge
engulfings in 1966. Every room full.

I am five. Nora May's long fuchsia
-veined fingers are on the *Goldflake*
packet, the heavy silver lighter clicking
as it sparks and goes out. From behind

the sofa, I hear the brandy loud
and thick as she talks of Bellevue, the
psychiatric patient who asked all night,
Is there a God? And who made him?

*All night, we couldn't stop her.*
*Is there a God? And who made him?*
*Is there a God? And who made him?*
*Goddamn, our heads were opening!*

*Two of us went in – wrapped*
*her in a sheet to the neck, filled*
*the bath to the top with cold –*
*No more out of her after that.*

*Is there a God? And who made him?*
Nora May picks fluff from her seamed
stockings, her long slim shinbone kicks out,
*Is there a God? And who made him?*

I am afraid someone will fill our
bath for her. I hold my breath.
One brother mentions the blackbird
and another nods, *Always before a death.*

They lower their lizard-wrinkled lids
over huge, once-beautiful eyes under
unnaturally black, unnaturally permed
and parted hair – Is there a God

and who made him?

## FINE GAEL FORM A COALITION WITH LABOUR, MARCH 1973

They never seemed close – the old whiskey
Master and the young pastel-lipped teacher.
They shared the same roof over our two-roomed
school, that was all – the dividing door a thick
50s coral gloss with its six panes of glass,
where their faces would appear if they needed
to summon one another. It wasn't often.
And she must have winced at the howls
that came from his side.
But when they met over his coffee flask
the day after the election, somehow
they couldn't separate. Fine Gael were *in!*
The party of professionals and well-heeled
farmers. Daddy's smile drew a line back to the
20s, to the Civil War, a victory for *The Big Fella*,
whose 8 by 4 photo stood on the mantelpiece
in Daddy's bedroom, Daddy's IRA
medal draped on one corner. I accepted it
then that such good news would drive people
to forget themselves but now I can't
believe the way they forgot us too –
what could the Master have been saying to her
that took so long, was he planning the budget
or choosing the cabinet of the 20th Dáil?
We weren't called in after the eleven o'clock break
we ran wild for miles, for hours, for weeks,
deep scratches along my thighs, Betty's old 60s
mini-dress with the pink and orange circles
no protection against the waist-deep briars
in the woods behind the church where everyone
who had them was smoking Carrolls No. 1.

We ransacked rubbish for makeshift hurleys –
anything would do, the boys said but
they banned my old frying pan when they saw
I could run forever with the ball.
I was wearing that light dress so it must
have been summer before it stopped.
All the beatings, the cruelty behind those walls
continued undisturbed but someone
had to put a stop to us roaming like tinkers
when boys were seen riding the roof
of Paddy the Priest's cottage like
it was a horse. And when Mick Looney
passed the graveyard, the crane shot
from his combine harvester showed him
a child on every stone.

# MOUNTAINY MEN

*Prologue*

*If you tell your dream, you don't have to dream it*
*any more*, says Alan Ladd, This Gun For Hire (1942).
I can tell you now I've tried it and it doesn't work.
It's your subconscious! Your subconscious, my eye!
They were just over-excited about Freud in the 40s.
Ingrid Bergman clucking over Gregory Peck in Spellbound (1945)
driving him mad with her fork on the white tablecloth.
Well, I, Johnny O'Hare, video-shop proprietor, (2008)
thought if I wrote it all down, I'd get those
girls out of my mind, that my sister Greta would
agree what the Ould Fella did, along with
Attracta, the skivvy, to our bed-ridden mother
& Blackie the cat & how we'd have been finished
if wasn't for Mrs Savage the Post Mistress.

I.

I'm not sentimental. That was cut out
of me early. That was the Ould Fella's
territory. The drink territory. At the
beginning we didn't know because
the Old Lady said it was Brucellosis.
The suffering was desperate, she said.
That was the rage & we were to have
the greatest pity because no one suffered
more than himself. Attracta came up
the mountain, rocking on the corks of her
white platforms, her purple-fringed handbag
knocking us out with her ould perfume called Styx.
May '76. Hotter than the Bronx.
Us all in a line at the kitchen table,
facing into his wonky six-feet big
kitchen window like the control
panel in Star Trek. All the stars.
Drinking tea under his 25-watt bulb,
Attracta's hand rattling the saucer.
Her big curls & out-sized eyes,
the Ould Fella's blue-black hand on the jamb
of the door, the keys of the powder-blue
Cortina over his callused wrist. She should
have buttoned up instead of casting
judgement on our window, you can't
go into a family home & start choosing
curtains for them.

2.

*Stuck to the bed for seven years* – to hear
the Ould Fella speak of the Old Lady
like that would make Blackie sick.
I nearly spewed my tea only I knew
even then how to button up. Greta had
her head craned looking at Attracta &
her perfume. Impressed. I wasn't.
We never had curtains on the Big Window.
The Ould Fella should have told Attracta
to skip it, but he grinned like a fool. He
was full of sucker talk after his naggin
& who was Attracta that he was trying
to impress? Attracta used to be known
as a *girl*. A *girl* could be any
age, basically a servant. Some were
treated rough. I heard the stories from people
coming into the shop. A *girl* could be
any age – as old as sixty. She might
be made to scrub a floor with a wooden
brush with no bristles. She might be made to
sleep in a shed & half-starved. She could be
attacked by the man of the house or the son
of the man of the house. *Girls* were dying
out in '76. They said Attracta
was too stupid to finish school. She was
hardly gone sixteen. I found out afterwards.

3.

The first night, Attracta swaying
on her stacked heels, pulling up her solferino
pop socks & going red while the Ould Fella –
after arranging a two-inch cream cuff
on his Wellington boots – couldn't get her
to look him in the eye. Long silences and
the only sound Blackie swallowing her
spit. Greta thought it was great
& took up swallowing her spit too.
She was stone mad for Blackie's plum-coloured
lips, lying down on the yard beside her,
waiting for her to yawn so that she could
look in at her magenta gums. She was staring
at Attracta's pop socks. *Count me absent*,
I said & took the stairs to the Old Lady.
Hot rainy evening & the continuous
questions, *Did Attracta admire the white lilac?*
*Did she say that blue and yellow daisies*
*were very unusual? I hope ye're making her*
*welcome. Is he able to keep his*
*temper?* She waited for Attracta to
come upstairs but she never came.

4.

I was savage with Greta, had she forgotten
the time she staggered in on the Old Lady's
abandoned stilettos and the Ould Fella
said he'd scourge her if he ever saw her
on high heels again? Now here was Attracta
wobbling all over the place like a
purple peril, he only spellbound
with the admiration and Greta
still with the marks from the old
scourging. He had every one of the Old Lady's
'50s and '60s costumes, hats, shoes, handbags
all locked into that woodworm wardrobe.
Greta rears up on me sometimes when
I ask her to put on the high heels because
Birkenstocks are very bad for business.
It ruins the look and especially for
tiny Veronica Lake. Noir women
rise and fall on their shoes, I keep telling her.
You only have to look at Barbara
Stanworth coming down the stairs –
in *Double Indemnity* (1944) – for God's sake.

5.

When I can't sleep, the only cure is to go
downstairs & put on a film. I've got an
Epsom Megaplex projector just for Greta
& myself alone. The black & white shadows
pass across the back wall of the parlour
that Greta's painted white. Bogey walks over
to light Bacall's fag or we're flying
ourselves, watching that helicopter shot
with Chickasaw, Bowie & T-Dub
in the farmer's jalopy after their breakout.
It helps me forget about the tormented *girls*.
I allowed a couple of special customers –
Jacky Tracey & Tommy Boyle –
in for our Saturday nights only I heard
them talking about me behind my back,
laughing at my violet gansey as if they
were some Sophisticatos themselves.
They said myself and the Ould Fella were
a pair of mules, one as bad as the other.
So was the end of their cinematic education.
They tried to crawl back but I told them skip it.
*Save that for some other mug,* I said.

6.

The old music. Deanna Durbin singing
*Always*, one big eye piercing out of the
shadows of the Lafitte. Or something from
the Sons of the Pioneers & John Ford
reminding me of Saturday afternoons
lying on Mrs Savage's Cadbury's wrapper
-coloured settee with Greta. *My Darling
Clementine*, (1948). That's where
I first saw *Shane* (1956).
Sometimes we long for a Rolo or a
Walnut Whip but that's for Saturday nights.
I won't say we haven't been tempted since
I got the popcorn, the Ben n Jerry's.
I had to. People renting DVDs
want to be vegetables, blown away from
reality with their gobs full but I'm still
the main attraction in my double-breasted
suit, cufflinks & pinky ring. *I didn't
believe you existed,* said one fella who'd
driven all the way from Limerick. Jerks.
99% per cent of the time; they'll
look at *They Live By Night* (1948)
or *A Colt is My Passport (*1967)
but say they're not in the mood for the old
black & white stuff, pick up *50 First Dates*
or *Gladiators,* a tub of M&M's, a barrel of
Coke, rush away on their bulbous trainers,
avoiding my eyes.

7.

I modelled myself on Alan Ladd because
I'm small & fair though I'd prefer Preminger's
dark Dana Andrews, policing himself for fear
he'd turn out be a hood like his old man –
*Where the Sidewalks Ends* (1950)
Or *Laura* (1944). All those fellows knew
how to hold it, how to button up.
Like de-mobbed WW2 soldiers –
they'd seen bad things, they'd done bad things.
They were men, they wouldn't talk.
Who could resist them? Greta wanted to be
Joan Bennett but she had to be Veronica Lake,
I said. She's pure Veronica like Veronica's risen
from the dead in her black velvet band.
People drive up the mountain to see us, our
polished library of noir. Me, in my grey fedora,
a small but fierce knowledgeable blonde fella,
Greta with her sharp shoulders & peak-
a-boo hair, working the sewing machine.

8.

Attracta's cup rattled on the saucer.
She pressed the bib of her puce dungarees
as if there was a button there or she
was checking her heart. Nerves. She must have been
uneasy. But she should have buttoned up.
No one asked her to ask questions or make
jokes. Why couldn't she say one right thing?
When Greta laughed, I gave her the nudge.
Of course the Ould Fella couldn't be stopped
laughing away like someone had asked him
for a can of laughter. & then he agreed to curtains
that would wipe out our big Star Trek window
that was a map of the sky every night to console
us in our troubles with a Brucellosis father
& a mother stuck to the bed all alone now –
this caper going on downstairs.

9.

Did the Old Lady know? She did but she
was buttoned up too. She was so buttoned
up she couldn't even have an illness
with a name. But she could hear their
voices rising with the lemon light shining
through the gaps of his crackpot floor. & the
queerness of the house didn't pass Attracta
by either. She said, *He must have been mad,
the fella who built this place.* & she
never said that again. The Ould Fella's face
went into a purple point. I thought it
might be the end of her. The Ould Fella
& his father built the house themselves out
of meanness. & because they were strangers
to the spirit level, everything was
at a wrong angle. They must have mislaid
the measuring tape too. The kitchen window
ended up six feet by four. To save glass they
made the rest of the windows into pure slits
like we were surrounded & going to have
to shoot arrows out of them.

10.

When the Ould Fella agreed to curtains,
I reported him to Mrs. Savage.
As Mitchum said – *Crossfire* (1947) –
the snakes were loose. The tightest man
in Knocklong hiring a girl when he was afraid
to spend a penny on anything except
his fancy shirts and he only had two of them
The lilac one with the white collar & the one
Mrs Savage said looked like Lemon Curd.
She thought he was a jerk, she didn't use
that word, she was too religious. She said
we were misfortunes when we broke
into the Post Office. She could have turned
us in. The Guard visited her every
Friday delivering pensions on his
Honda 50, looking for wild children.
He asked for names. The Kellehers snorted
inside their anoraks as if they knew
& might tell any minute. I saw him throw
his eye at me from the side of his cap.
But we were only after the Light
because Himself opened every ESB bill
with a roar of rage like he was stung &
every room in the house was purple with the
shadows of a twenty-five watt bulb except for
the pitch-black loft where we slept.

II.

The day of the Heist, I had Greta primed
to vomit – she could do it at the drop
of a hat – during the hour of Mrs Savage's
Erin Oxtail Soup. No one disturbed
the Post Office then because Mrs Savage
was well got & it was right in the middle
of Catechism. *Does God see us? God sees*
*us for nothing is hidden from his all-*
*seeing eye. Does God know all things? God knows*
*all things, past, present & to come, even our*
*most secret thoughts & actions.* I led Greta
by the hand through the green iron gate
of the school with the smell of vomit off her.
Would we see the face of the priest or his
interrogation buckteeth on the road?
I didn't want it at all but Greta
was having nightmares even in the day
she was so scared of the night. I could hear
Greta swallowing her spit like Blackie
as we flew past the priest's house, his hydrangeas
in bloom – big pink & blue heads on them.
We were lucky. We met no one.

12.

Greta's face was blue-white with the fear
& excitement of getting inside. She wanted to be
Post Mistress. That was the job all the small
girls were after. Nothing else would do them.
The Post Office was down in a hollow
growing out of the ground like a mushroom
with a green wooden door *Oifig an Phoist*
& a spray of pink roses over the door.
The girls were mad to be at all the stuff.
The books of stamps & the tearing along
the dotted line & the lump of red wax
that Mrs Savage had to melt over
the brown paper label tying the neck
of the sack of letters before the man
in the van came for them every day at
four o clock. She had a crowd of us watching
her at four when she lit a red match &
put it to the wax. You heard nothing only
her breath.

13.

Mrs Savage had Bobby bars & Lunches
& Scrumbles & Catches. Aztecs, McGowan's
toffee & Calypso bars, Pineapple Splits,
Raspberry splits & Banana ones &
the stuff she weighed into small white paper bags –
 Pineapple Chunks, Rum & Butters, Malt n' Creams,
Acid Drops, Scots Clan & Quality Street.
Everything shone in the glass jars.
The balls of chewing gum – Sour Grape, Cherry
& Orange. Krojak pops. The clean gluey
sealing-wax smell mixed with
toffee & Cadbury's milk chocolate.
We were supposed to be getting bicycle
lamp batteries but when Greta pointed &
I picked up two Banana Splits & some Flogs
& a handful of Black Jacks, I couldn't stop.
There was an overpowering smell of melting toffee,
& the sweet nutty smell of the old yellow
library books I read to the Old Lady. I lost it,
went jingle-brained, tore the wrapper
off the banana split, crammed the whole thing
into my mouth, a painful point sticking out
of my cheek. Greta copied me, our mouths
so full they hurt. I was trying
to get a grip, to rib myself up for
what we were there for – double bicycle-lamp
batteries below the big roll of shining
brown paper – when we heard the awful
clitter of the dog's toenails on the shiny lino.
She, of course, was silent on her rubber soles.

14.

As one, we threw our sweets to the floor,
Greta thudding the penny bars.
The small voice *Can I help ye?* wouldn't be
heard above a clothesline, Mrs Savage,
standing in her navy housecoat, tight-laced
white nurses' shoes, her two blue eyes twice
the size because of her thick pink glasses.
Her crown of silver plaits. Jacky, the Jack
Russell clipped out on the lino & looked
at us too & a bee buzzed inside an empty
bottle of Fanta Orange. Mrs Savage wiped her lips
with a tea towel with carrots on it, waited.
I knew pronto I had to be on the level.
I said we'd come for the light. Your
poor mother. Mrs Savage put down the
towel & I wanted to say, *I don't*
*want your damn pity* – only I couldn't.
Of course, we ended up great with each
other. The Ould Fella tried but he couldn't
keep us away from the Post Office after that.

15.

The Old Lady lay in bed, reading library
books. Greta couldn't & I could hardly
remember a time when she was out of the bed.
The Ould Fella went bananas trying
to find the cure. He brought up Billy Lyons –
to stand at the foot of the bed, smelling of
Clark's No 1. Plug – because Billy
was supposed to be the seventh son of a
seventh son & had hidden knowledge.
*Hidden knowledge!* said Mrs Savage, *the
only thing Billy Lyons knows is who
went up the road & down & what time &
how many times.*

## 16.

Mrs Savage's friend, Irene Cassidy
cleaned for a Mrs Barry in Cork who knew a
jockey whose head had been squashed by a horse.
He turned into a healer after he cured himself
but was very select who he'd take.
Irene asked Mrs Barry to ask him
and it was all set up when the Ould Fella
roared at the two of them, *Mother of God
are ye demented or what?* I said, *No Quacks!*
He was mauve with the rage & the two women
were boiling too because the jockey was
very put out & Irene had to face Mrs Barry
on Monday morning. The Ould Fella's mauve
complexion broke up into pink & purple
lozenges floating across his face like
swirls of gas passing over the planet Mars.
*A jockey, is it? Oh, we're not as bad
as that yet.*

17.

He was desperate every evening
standing at the foot of the stairs listening
hoping she might rise like Lazarus,
go back to the pile of puce chiffon she
left on the sewing machine in '68.
And he was a briar to myself & Greta –
he said everyone was leaning on him,
lying down reading library books in
a filthy house. But we knew when we heard
the unscrewing of the cap on the naggin
we could relax even if he was annoying –
quoting from poems he learned at school –
like an edjit, like Alan Mowbray drunk
in My Darling Clementine (1948).
*The Beauty of this world hath made me sad,*
*this beauty that will pass*, he said to Greta
& then he'd go back to the bottom of
the stairs again, *Mon grá do daingeann thú*
*an la do fhaca thú!* calling out to the Old Lady
I loved you from the day I saw you,
kneeling to trace every old stiletto
pock mark she left on the lino floor.
She never answered. & then one day
he went into the doctor & he came
back with a name. Dr. Jones, he said.
*He's after curing a load of them*, he put
the naggin to his lips. *A load of what?*
asked Greta. *A load of woman*, he said.

18.

*Our troubles are over,* the Ould Fella
said while we waited for Dr Jones.
Greta was drawing on a brown paper
bag on the table under the Star Trek
window. *He's after fixing a load of them.*
His black eyes bored into the purple darkness
between the white lilacs as Dr Jones
came into view, fierce determined-looking,
a leather bag in one hand & a torch in the other.
When his combover blew up and stood at right angles
to his head like a galvanized sheet quivering
in the wind, the Ould Fella cried out,
*Mother of God what kind of a gowl is*
*O'Connor after sending me?* He sent
Dr. Jones to the porch to fix his hair.
*Do you want to frighten her to death?*
Dr. Jones's white chin floated
in the dark like a bar of Lux soap.
I was afraid he'd turn back but he went
on up the stairs with his bag like a doctor
in a film. And then the Ould Fella
threw his head on table & groaned. He said
he'd been had & t'would kill him to pay.
He couldn't bear it. What was keeping Jones
so long? He ran up the stairs & ran down
again, shouting. He'd been ordered out of
his own bedroom where he hadn't been allowed
to sleep for six years & Dr. Jones was
not doing a tap, apart from trying
to hypnotize the Old Lady with her
own Biro that she used for doing the
crosswords.

19.

Dr Jones pointed his bar-of-soap chin
at the Ould Fella, *There is the business*
*of an invoice & I can't possibly take*
*a cheque.* Determined to get his lettuce.
The Ould Fella told him to feck off with himself –
cash or cheque was going to make no difference –
because he was paying no bill for no man
swinging a Biro. Jones said he wanted
his cash right on the barrelhead. The Ould
Fella took off his jacket & roared *Quack!*
Did Jones want a faceful of knuckles?
At that, myself & Greta were forty
miles an hour up the stairs to the Old Lady's
bedroom. It must have been a quick scuffle
because we were only in time to see
the end of it out the narrow window –
the Ould Fella slapping Jones's car, *G'wan*
*out of that with your Grievous Bodily Harm!*
He was still shouting when he came upstairs.
He'd have Jones in court for fraud. He'd stolen
the Old Lady's Biro. The Old Lady
clung to Greta, her face as white as the wall.
*There's no fear is there, that he'd bring back*
*the Guards?*

20.

The Ould Fella blamed Mrs Savage –
she'd addled him with her talk of Quacks.
So when she wanted to give me a job wiping
& stacking shelves, he roared a big Brucellosis
*No!* at her & said I should be at home looking after
my mother & sister. Mrs Savage squeezed
her blue eyes behind her pink glasses,
*Ah we were looking forward & Greta*
*was going to sit on my little high*
*stool cutting the tops off the Cork Examiners.*
The stool was made of golden wood & not
very high with a sky-blue leather cover.
Mrs Savage rubbed the seat like she wanted
Greta to jump up on it like a Jack
Russell herself. The Ould Fella couldn't
stand that. He said, *Didn't I say no?*
*They have to take care of Mary.* His face
was as hard as the end of a spade. *God,*
are they taking care of Mary & they
*as young as that?* The Ould Fella laughed,
Sure weren't you about to put them to work
*yourself a minute ago?* & he walked
out quick with the last word & a smile like
a painted moustache.

21.

He put the bite on Irene Cassidy
after Mass. He must have been off his nut.
I thought he wasn't talking to Irene
after the jockey but he told me that
it was only Mrs. Savage that he
was bucking with. *It's the ould ones who do
the interfering. The young ones are better
& they know how to work.* Irene Cassidy
was standing by Father Twomey's grave in
her cream gloves & coffee-coloured trouser
suit, talking to old Mrs Mahoney
who was admiring her olive-skinned girls
in their Aran jumpers. *Aren't they handsome
to the world?* Mrs Mahoney was loud because
she was deaf & the Ould Fella bored his eyes
into her.

22.

The Cassidys were like models because
Irene made her living out of knitting
Aran jumpers for Yanks after Travellers
had murdered her husband, the gambler.
The whole parish never stopped admiring
her & saying that she could turn her hand
to anything & wasn't she great, the widow.
Irene said that she'd do it all again
with the husband. She loved nothing better
than knitting especially the blackberry design.
They loved that, the sentimental fools.
I remembered Cassidy's gold flashing
in his mouth, next door to a Traveller himself,
a grifter, a three-time loser. Easy for Irene
to be handing out sucker talk when she
knew the low-life could never come back.
The Cassidys' faces were puce from the heat
of their blackberry-encrusted jumpers.
They stared at the Ould Fella. It was very
embarrassing the way he went barreling
in, putting his fat back to old Mrs
Mahoney, *Irene, I'm in desperate need
of help.*

23.

The Ould Fella drew Irene up the road.
I was tailing because I could see he
was getting complicated. Hurry up,
I said to the Cassidys. *Isn't it
glorious weather?* Irene was nervous
but the Ould Fella was having no small
talk, only lowering his voice, his head
like a bull, so I couldn't hear a word
he was saying. Irene touched her lip with
her cream glove. When she pulled it away
she looked annoyed at the red lipstick stain.
The two children started humming.
Shh, Shh, I said & then I heard him say,
*There's children at stake. I've said it,* she raised
her voice, *I have no time to help you.* &
*Mother of God,* he said, kicking gravel
in his excitement, *that was the last thing
on my mind.* They were outside the Post Office
now & Mrs Savage's pink & blue face
came to that small window divided into
eight squares by the green wooden frame, *The cost
of a girl,* the Ould Fella shouted. Three
wavy lines appeared on Irene's forehead.
She pointed her red-stained glove over to
the low wall beside the priest's house where
Attracta sat on her own, eating a banana
wafer ice-cream.

24.

Has she mentioned the lilacs? The Old Lady
wanted to know, lying back with the window
open in the evening, swallowing great
draughts of that smell but not enjoying it
one bit any more. Still no sign of Attracta.
What if she was frightened with a strange man?
It wasn't everyone that knew about
the Rage of Brucellosis. She'd hardly
spoke when laughter bubbled up through the pale
yellow cracks of light in the floorboards. She
asked me to read from *The Queen's Confession*.
The Old Lady was desperate sorry
for Marie Antoinette. The poor girl stripped
at the border & then all alone in
a foreign court! The spending, the necklace,
the revolution, Count Axel Von Fersen
& the big conspicuous green escape
coach with the red wheels & white velvet seats.
The highlight was The Execution.

Marie Antoinette's mother, Empress
of Austria had the snap on the whole
of Europe & was always sending her
instructions. *The only real happiness
in this world comes from a happy marriage.
I can say this from experience. And
all depends on the woman, who should be
willing, gentle & able to amuse.*
The Old Lady's eyes were violet in the light
from the orange plastic lamp. *Wasn't that
hard, Johnny? Didn't Marie Antoinette
have it hard?* She asked me to read again
about the last time Marie Antoinette
saw her father. *His servants were watching,
& abruptly he signed to one of them to
take me from him. He turned to his friends who
were beside him & said in a voice, shaken
with emotion: 'Gentlemen, God knows how
much I desired to kiss that child'.* I was afraid
she'd start talking about her own father
because he was a saint & it was very boring
but she just wiped her eyes & told me
to turn out the light.

## 26.

The next day I thought I'd had it.
I couldn't climb that stairs to her again.
The Ould Fella & Attracta were examining
two scrawny brown hens in the yard.
The Ould Fella saying he could get more for her.
I stood paralysed to the lino with my hands
in my pockets. The Star Trek window was
full of the purple mountains & the smell
of lilac was sickening. The Old Lady called,
*Johnny, Johnny, darling are you there?* Greta
was drawing on the inside of a cornflakes packet
as if I was the only one in the house who had
hearing. & still I was stuck to the floor,
with the creamery clock doing my nut.
I wanted her to just get out of that bed.
None of the helpless pulling up against
the bed covers & falling back down.
Just get up quick smart like a someone might
if a boy ran out to the hallway & shouted *Fire!*
Up the stairs. Because that's what I felt like doing.

27.

Someone had to get a grip though.
Someone had to. & then the Old Lady said
she didn't think she should see Attracta herself.
*Sure, I'm in an awful state, I'll have to put*
*on some weight. I'll have to go on the Guinness.*
She was delirious to think Guinness
was going to pull her out now but
every night the Ould Fella brought her a glass
of Guinness sweetened with six spoons of sugar
& she was gagging it down. The sound of the
swallowing & the faces she was making!
I stayed at my post, reading The Queen's Confession:
*So he went to the opera & was*
*taken ill there. He had a stroke & died*
*in Leopold's arms. It was naturally*
*said afterwards that he, being near death,*
*had had a terrible premonition*
*of my future & that was why he had*
*sent for me in that unusual manner.*
The Old Lady said she'd never get over
it, the sadness of that. A young girl like that
being sent alone to the French court with
no protection.

28.

Someone should have knocked sense into him –
said, *You're wearing the wrong lipstick, Mister.*
Attracta was doing all the cleaning
like she was Housewife of the Year, Patron
Saint of the Bucket & Mop, as if Greta
& I hadn't been doing a tap all along.
Clattering around importantly
in a pair of fat American scuffs,
she'd pull out a big lump of dirt & fluff
from some mad place like behind the fridge where
you had to have dirt & say, *Will you take
one look at that!* He nodded away as if
he was the Chief Inspector, the Patron
Saint of Cleaners. In the evening he wore
maroon suede slip-ons, swinging them as he
sat on the old Volkswagen seat in front
of the fire. & then Attracta started
her blackening of the reputation
of the poor cat.

29.

Attracta said she didn't like the way
that Blackie was looking at her.
She couldn't stand the way Blackie swallowed
her spit. She didn't say that Greta was
copying Blackie, Greta said but she felt
Attracta was thinking it. I was with
the Old Lady reading about ominous
foreboding, *I have an ominous foreboding*
*that the Captain isn't long for this life.*
I had ominous foreboding when
I passed through the kitchen, the two eyeing
each other over Greta's head bent over
her sheet of brown paper. I thought I'd do
a bit of cleaning myself & I went
into the porch which was as cold as a slug's
belly even in the height of that summer.
I started polishing our school shoes.
I put elbow grease into it.
*The Captain is not long for this life,* I said.

30.

The Ould Fella said we weren't *respecting*
Attracta. She'd complained about my black looks.
Respect. Was she the bishop that we had
to kneel & kiss her ring? I should have watched
over Greta but I had to mind the Old Lady &
I wasn't Blessed Martin De Porres.
I couldn't bi-locate. I told Greta to keep away
from them & Blackie too but while I was upstairs
reading *Gone With the Wind*, Attracta complained
again that Blackie was staring at her &
got the Ould Fella to put the poor creature outside.
They might as well have driven a stake through
Greta's heart.

31.

Blackie was no sooner outside than
she had herself pressed against
the Star Trek window staring in, her
gold eyes as big & bright as the headlamps
on tractors. Attracta said the cat was
putting her heart crossways with the flashing
lights at the window & that we'd have to
get curtains now. The Ould Fella banged on
the starry glass. Blackie disappeared &
Greta started crying only Attracta
cried louder. The Old Lady asked, *Do you
hear raised voices?* When I went down Greta
was gone to the loft. *Bed is the only
place for that one*, said the Ould Fella, he
was watching the television. Attracta
was lining the cupboards with pink wallpaper,
her red eyes looking away from me, &
I said, *What?* & The Ould Fella said, *Shh
the news is on. The news.*

## 32.

The fridge groaned in the porch &
I went in there & saw Blackie with her
mouth open against the glass, calling to me so
I went out into the yard & I carried her
back in holding her tight. I had to. She was
tearing into me. That was natural, she was a cat.
I struggled up to the loft with my bleeding hands.
But I couldn't get into the bed because Greta'd
turned the bicycle lamps off & I couldn't find
the opening in the tent we'd made around the bed
with blankets for the cold. It was Blackie who
found the opening snorting like a horse to
get to Greta. I whispered *Take no notice of that rip,*
*we'll get rid of Attracta yet* & Greta whispered
*You're frightening me!* I'd frightened myself.
My raspy voice coming out of the darkness like that.
My hands were stinging with the scratches.
Greta asked me if her hair had gone white overnight
like Marie Antoinette's. She sat up in the bicycle lamp
light & the shadows fell over the top of her head
like she was wearing a black helmet. Like a samurai.
Now she was frightening *me*. But I stayed cool.
Told her if she lay down and kept her yap
shut, we'd all be hunky dory.

Mrs Savage said that the Ould Fella was
in no position to point the finger.
She had Campbell's Cream of Tomato soup
for us every day after school. We stayed
until Mary Tyler Moore was over
& went there again to watch Westerns on
Saturday afternoons. Mrs. Savage
said the cheek of Attracta wanting to
put up curtains in a family home.
Mrs Savage said that Attracta was so
slow, she was dangerous. & she said it
was a fright to God that the wrong people
had the children. Sometimes she made us Cream
of Celery with a drop of sherry in it. That
was from *Woman's Own*. & she cut Calvita
cheese into matchsticks & criss-crossed them on
cream crackers. We knew she wanted us.
She showed us the two blue beds in the room.
I chopped her wood with a Mitchum stroke
& Greta played with her box of Christmas
decorations. Little red-breasted robins &
blue ones & mauve & snow white ones.
Mrs Savage always held Greta just
before we left & Jacky barked with the
jealousy.

34.

Attracta wore earrings with hoops so wide
the Ould Fella joked that Blackie could have
jumped through them, Attracta shivered & looked
at Blackie & said, *The dirty thing.* Five
minutes later myself & Greta
followed her into the porch where we saw her
throw a kick at the cat. Greta ran to the loft
with Blackie struggling in her arms.
*What did she ever do to you?* I said, throwing
a kick back at her. I hit Bull's Eye, her shin cracked
& she was crying again that it was fright to God
that the two of us hated her & she was after
killing herself, cleaning up after us. *Hadn't ye the
dirtiest house in the parish before I came?*
I said I'd tell the Ould Fella what she said
& she said she'd tell him herself. She should
never have left her home place. *And aren't ye
all stupid from Island?* I said and we ran off.

## 35.

The Ould Fella appeared outside the barn
at the top of the yard as I was looking through
the purple glass wrapper of a Quality Street.
I saw Attracta coming out of the house
with something on the end of a broom.
More dirt to be holding against us.
She went up to the top of the yard &
I watched them talking. I nearly dropped
when she gave him a big shove & I thought
at last. She's for the Brucellosis now but
he was only laughing when he pushed her
into the barn. The one red barn door was flapping
so much with the force of their entry that the
old brown hen was nearly decapitated
with the burst of the door coming back.
It tore squawking down the yard to me
to where I stood winded in a purple haze.

36.

I made for the stairs after that I was afraid
the Old Lady might have seen something
& she had because she was leaning against
the iron bedstead looking through the bars
like Marie Antoinette in La Conciergerie.
Once I started I couldn't stop. I don't know
how long it went on with the Old Lady
stroking my head & telling me to Take No
Notice of Nobody & Don't let Daddy hear you.
When he came back in, he came up the stairs
to me. The Old Lady hung on to me.
He shouted *Come out of that!* My eyes were
so squeezed up from crying, I couldn't see
her but he was as clear as if he'd been
outlined with Magic Marker. He said, *You've
upset your mother.* I called him a gowl.
I put my fists up but I was too small.
Fair & delicate like Greta & the Old Lady.
He belted me down the stairs & I called him
the Coward of the County & he said
I was a cry baby & when he was
finished, he put me sitting on the step
outside the back door.

## 37.

I woke up like a bunged-up barrelhouse vag.
Looking out the narrow slit of our window,
I saw Attracta in a white dress
in the front of the house. She was doing
her exercises, tipping her toes. She can't
see us, I said & we stuck our tongues out
& then she stuck hers back at us so we
couldn't go down for breakfast after that.
We dressed fast. I plaited Greta's hair like I did every
morning since the Old Lady's sight started
going. As a September fog came down
like an ominous foreboding we fell
against a Traveller's caravan with
a slitty-eyed child hung upside calling
us mountainy men. Advancing in, we shouted
at it. We couldn't see if it was a boy or a girl –
the blood was in its head. *Shut up, you!* I said.
A tall man with black side-locks &
a blackberry-stained handkerchief appeared.
I couldn't understand his husky voice. Greta said
he was calling us weasels so we backed
away up the road but my stomach
was turned. I threw my bread & jam on the
tarmac & the crows came down like buzzards.
We were an hour early for school so we played
45 on the grassy ditch & spades were trumps
when I realised we'd forgotten to
say goodbye to the Old Lady.

38.

School was Calvary with the bruises.
The Master asked me if I'd got my
Come-Uppance & third, fourth, fifth &
sixth class all laughed in a chorus. We were
all in the one room. I played the Tough Guy
& put a Biro in my mouth like it
was a fag until he told me to take it out.
It drizzled all day. Damp smells came in drifts.
Breadcrumbs & milk from the lunches. I was
cold until we got to the Post Office
& then I got hot. Too hot when Mrs
Savage saw my face full of knuckles, He's
been in to say that ye left for school
without his permission. *Now I know why.*
She threatened to call the guards, the black phone
held against her silver crown only Greta
started crying so she stopped & gave
us Double Centres but then she worried
again. She said it wasn't right & she
held Jacky so tight against her white shopcoat,
he gave a piercing shriek.

## 39.

Mrs Savage got tough but I was no rat.
I thought she wasn't either. The questions
were like having a pitchfork poked into me.
I writhed around the chair, acting a bit
hoping she'd let me off, but she only
gave me both barrels, I know I promised
not to say a word to the Guards but that
was because I thought you were going
to tell me everything. She was crazy.
Would you see Robert Mitchum or Alan
Ladd running down the road to the Post Office
with their mouths flapping? Okay. I told about
the curtains but The Guards were another Kettle
of Fish. I sat there while the sun went round the back
of the Post Office & the small stumpy windows
were black in the shadow. The same as it is today
the shadows of roses like black
heads nodding beside the shelves of film.
She took me upstairs, showed me
our two blue beds again & we came down
the tiny staircase so tight next to the ceiling,
we had to duck our heads. I had my hands
in my trousers pockets the whole time. The
black thorny branch of the rose knocked against
the small windowpane. I wouldn't talk.

40.

Mrs Savage burnt her old rosary beads
& a prayer book that swelled
after being left out in the rain. You were allowed
on the night of St John's Eve. She let Greta
poke the hot pink embers through the silver
bars of her range before we walked home.
The lovely smell of turf & the blazing
St John's fires began to disappear as
we got near Knocklong. The Ould Fella
hadn't lit one since the Old Lady took
to her bed. Greta had hold of my arm.
We took a detour to avoid the Travellers
though we heard scuffling in the ditch & we
didn't know if it was them or an animal.
We turned into the yard at half past eight.
The Ould Fella stood in the doorway in
his turned-down wellingtons smoking a fag.
*Well, I know where ye were,* he said with his
blue-black chin. Mrs Savage gave us Double
Centres, Greta said. *Oh I'm sure she gave
ye Double Centres, the witch!* The Ould Fella
took a pitchfork & went off up the yard, big
shadows bouncing from him.

Attracta was gone, leaving a smell of
Mansion Polish behind her & the big
window so shining & clear as it began to go
purple & black outside. I felt I could
reach out & touch all the planets.
*That's the plough up there,* the Ould Fella
used to point and I'd stare at his pink hand
with the black hairs that looked like flies on his fingers.
I was so nervous, nodding my head up & down,
*Yes, Yes,* concentrating so hard on looking
that I couldn't see a blind thing beyond
his hand. But I saw it that night. For some reason,
it was as clear and cold as an icy wheelbarrow.
Greta was petting Blackie who was thrown down
on the table groaning & stretching her legs
when I remembered the Old Lady. I called as
I went up the stairs but there was no answer
only a blast of heat when I shoved open the door.
He'd the fire lighting for her & she was asleep
& snoring. Mogadon said the label
on the bottle of pills on the table.
I rattled them. Greta came behind me
& rattled them too & I said, *Will you
stop doing everything I do?* I asked her
*Have you ever in your whole life heard
the Old Lady snoring?*

42.

I tried to close her mouth & when we came
out of her bedroom Greta couldn't find
Blackie to take to bed with us. Greta
got a pain in her stomach & I made
us two glasses of Andrews Liver Salts.
Greta slept but I got a pain in
my stomach. All the things Mrs Savage
said whirled round me like a San Francisco
fog round Humphrey Bogart. Blackie
was missing in the morning. Greta went
up & down the yard calling and crying
Even Attracta went out, hitting the
yellow tin tray, calling *Blackie, Blackie*
& clicking her tongue as if she was a dog.
Attracta'd a guilty conscience. She put
pink cake in our school bags & the Ould
Fella had his painted moustache smile. When
I tried to go upstairs to say goodbye
to the Old Lady, he was in my way,
stamping down the corner of the lino
where it curled up on the first step.
He said not to go up, to let her sleep on.

43.

I knew when I heard the knock during
Catechism. *How will the bodies of the
damned rise? The bodies of the damned will not
rise glorious, but they will be immortal, to share
in the everlasting punishment of the soul.*
That's where we were at in the Green
Catechism when Mrs Savage arrived
with her watering blue eyes behind her
pink glasses, her silver crown slightly
to one side. I wonder now if she moved it
for effect, looking back on that cottage &
the way everything was arranged.
She told us to get our coats. The Old Lady
had died of pneumonia. God rest her soul.
The Master said nothing, only scratched his
Brillo-haired head & stroked his long
yellow teeth with his Parker pen. Mrs Savage
said he knew no better.

44.

Mrs Savage made tinned salmon sandwiches.
They curled untouched on her willow plate.
Greta drank Lucozade. I can still
hear it fizzling. Mrs Savage filling up
the ruby tumbler. Hardly another
sound except for Jacky who'd something stuck
in his foot. He was gnawing at it.
Mrs Savage looked, pushing the pads apart
until he cried out but she never found anything.
Even liquid stuck in my guilty throat.
I hammered into Sour Grapes chewing gum
until my jaw locked at half past eight.
Our first night there. She made her own
lavender curtains out of thin material.
Greta calls it calico. They used it
for sewing in school. You could see roses
dancing on their stems outside & all
the flowers on the material
stand out as if travelling on the air.
It still lets the light in today.

## 45.

We refused to look at the body. I didn't
mean to but I was afraid I might vomit.
Greta was looking for Blackie who hadn't
been thinking about anything except her own
comfort the whole time according to the
The Ould Fella. She'd been lying on the stone
hearth in the Old Lady's room soaking up
all the heat she could on St John's night.
That was how she got locked into the room.
He whispered behind Greta's back
asking me did I not think it was the sign
of a very unhealthy cat to be thrown down
like that by a fire when any strong-blooded
creature would be roaming the fields of
a summer's night? I shook, remembering
how he taken off up the yard with his
pitchfork on St John's Eve. Greta flung herself
on the cat, roaring, *I love you, I love
you, I love you.* Blackie struggled to get away.
Relations came, we never saw before or since,
old men with hooky noses from the Old Lady's side
a couple of nuns from the Ould Fella's side,
*God bless the Mark* they said. There was the smell
of candles & the Colman's Mustard that
Mrs Mahoney & Mrs Savage were slapping
on the ham sandwiches & against my will –
I didn't think it was right – my appetite
came back.

# 46.

The biggest land was when he opened
the woodworm wardrobe and Attracta
started parading to Mass in the Old Lady's
costumes – the café au lait suit, the two-tone
cream and chocolate pumps, even the stilettos
when they were away out of fashion.
And hadn't Father Twomey said over his dead
body should pointy shoes be allowed to ruin
the terraza floor? And it was over
his dead body, wasn't he outside
in the church graveyard himself? I thought
it was desperate bad luck but Mrs Savage
said that Attracta wasn't *as cracked as she
lets on* and the way Mrs Savage said that
gave me the shivers. It gave Greta the
shivers too. We lay in bed on either
side of Blackie holding her to the mattress
in case she took off. Our hearts bursting
out of our suffocating chests every night –
would the two of them to come out of
the dark with a pillow to smother us?
Attracta complained again that I was
giving her black looks & he said he didn't
want to hear any more ould guff out of me
& that I wasn't to be giving Attracta
*instructions*. I said that there was supposed
to be no decorating done in any
house for twelve months after a funeral.
But Attracta had the material
bought. A big bolt of wine velvet, as
Mrs Savage said – not suitable for a kitchen at all,
more like a bishop's cloak.

47.

Between the curtains & the rifling through
the sacred treasures of the woodworm wardrobe,
there were snakes everywhere we looked.
Wasn't it just outside Mass where the Old Fella
saw Attracta first? & she was inside Mass now
which was only a fashion parade as everyone
knew. Always. Sure, when the Old Lady read us
*Fair, Brown and Trembling* where did Trembling
appear in her finery? It was no ball, I can tell you
for the Irish Cinderella. *She* appeared at Mass.
& whatever about all the cleaning and skivvying,
Attracta was no Trembling. Trembling didn't have
to steal her special *shoes with the toes red, the middle white,*
*and the backs and heels green.* Because she was good.
& Attracta was so bad, digging into that terrazza
floor with her orchid heels, we thought Father
Twomey might rise up out of his grave in a pillar
of black smoke. I was hoping he would.

48.

The Travellers were parked on the road again,
we had to walk to school through the fields
to avoid them. Attracta slept in the Old
Lady's room because she was afraid to
go home she said but she should be more afraid
of a ghost's vengeance, said Mrs Savage.
She said that their carry on was a mortal sin.
She was afraid we might be sent to an orphanage.
There's a baby on the way, Greta heard Mrs Savage
saying to Irene Cassidy & we wanted her
to take us now before it was too late only
Greta heard Mrs Savage saying something
to Irene Cassidy about being too old to adopt
she was on tablets for her heart & she
could hardly breathe with the asthma. We
nearly died in the loft with the anxiety,
awake all night imagining her
keeling over from breathlessness.

49.

Greta was going out of her mind about
Blackie and Blackie took advantage.
Became very demanding. Four exciting meals
a day was what she was after. Imagine
trying to do that on top of a County
Cork mountain in '76? Alan Ladd
got it wrong in This Gun for Hire (1942)
when he said cats were on their own,
didn't need anybody. I never
saw a cat yet that didn't make a fool
out of Greta. I had to put a stop
to them after the last fella died.
They say Harvey Keitel
was handed two pages of dialogue once
& he tossed it away – *I can say all this
just by the way I stand,* says he. Well, Harvey
was a sap compared with Blackie. *She* could
speak volumes just lying in a lump.

50.

Attracta baked Queen Cakes every day &
wore an apron but there was no point sucking
up to us. The Ould Fella & herself
were in a jam. The eyes of the parish on them.
Mrs Savage said we were not to be taken in
with any plámás. She hugged Greta so tight
that Jacky started scratching her housecoat
as well as barking with the jealousy.
I didn't need Mrs Savage to tell
me this. Underneath the sweet smell of baking
was a horrible cabbagey one. Attracta
couldn't stop boiling dishcloths & stirring
the pot with a wooden spoon. Anyone with
eyes in their head could see what she was.

51.

The wind whipped through the telephone wires.
The four of us jumping at every shadow,
especially our own ones. & there were plenty
of shadows because of the low wattage of the bulbs.
I'd go up to the loft every night with Greta
& Blackie, vowing that I wouldn't come down
before morning. We took a jug of water
but I'd drink the lot & have to come down
again with the raging thirst. I was in
my socks that Saturday evening when I
saw the two of them swirling round the floor
to The Blue Danube on Radio Eireann.
Two months after the Old Lady died.
His fat back in his lilac shirt. I would
have said I didn't care what he said but
when he said, *I always wanted a son*, I
drew a line, stood there accusing them.
But they were blind as they moved around
in front of the big dark blue window shining
– like a well we were all going to drown in.

52.

We ate in the bedroom, Cream Crackers
& Calvita. Greta cut the cheese into
matchsticks & criss-crossed them. The Ould Fella
roared up at us a couple of times to
Come down out of that but I didn't want
to look at him. Greta said she didn't either.
We came down at night for food & the only
way we'd leave the house was by climbing out
of the slit of the bedroom window & on to
the porch with a rope to the ground.
Mrs Savage told us to keep our powder dry.
One night we heard him telling Attracta
he had to patrol the boundaries. We watched
him going up the yard & then we heard her
singing *Her eyes, they shone like diamonds, you'd
think she was Queen of the Land.* She was
standing on the window sill, hanging wine
velvet, the Old Lady hardly in her grave & she
singing *The Black Velvet Band.*

53.

I always wanted a son. What was I? A fairy?
I stood behind Attracta & the stars
were as clear & sharp as knives.
I put the jug down on the table. I think
I wanted to listen. She was good singer,
*with her hair slung over her shoulder, wrapped*
*up in a black velvet band.* & then well
I didn't push. I just took a step forward
& she screamed. I put my hands out
but she flew. Up & out through the glass
with the pins in her mouth, the material in her hands.
Glass everywhere and I was running through it.
Up the stairs, slipping & flopping
in my stockinged feet like a seal. I thought
I'd never get to the top to where Greta was
standing, her face as white as a daisy,
the bicycle lamp tight in her hands.

54.

In the loft, I couldn't speak. I asked Greta
to read to me. Her breath was sweet with
Cream Crackers. The heat of the summer
was gone by now & we were feeling the cold
so we put the rug from the floor on top
of ourselves & the dust made us sneeze.
She read *The Tale of Samuel Whiskers*.
Big fat fella thrown down giving orders
to a pure jade known as Anna Maria.
The two of them would put the heart
crossways in anyone & Mother of God,
the way he said to Maria, *Make me a
kitten dumpling roly-poly pudding*
while Tom Kitten was lying there, all tied
up with string terrified me. *Don't make
it with pastry make it with breadcrumbs*,
I can still see Anna Maria, her narrow back
bent forward, darting off to get the butter.

55·

I didn't want to go back down.
I didn't want to see her telegraphing
me with her Joan Crawford eyes but he was
shouting *Help, help, help ye fucking
bastards,* so we had to. I told Greta to stand back.
I wouldn't look at Attracta. I kept my eyes on
the holly bush beside her. I kicked at a weed.
I saw her shoe, lying bruised & pointed.
He looked at me looking. *Go down to Mooney's
yard & tell them to call the Guards.* Greta
wanted to go with me because she knew
I'd have to pass the Travellers caravan
but he held her back. *Johnny's well able for
it,* he said. *That fella's able for anything.*

## 56.

After the ambulance left, he hammered boards
over the Big Window & it was dark, day
& night. We thought we'd be there forever,
creeping around in the mauve shadows
eating Marietta biscuits in the loft, washing
them down with Andrews Liver Salts.
But he gave in in the end, like Mrs Savage
said he would if we kept our powder dry.
After a week, he brought the blue Cortina round
the side of the house & we packed up.
Greta held Blackie on the back seat
with the sewing machine. Blackie was crying
& scratching all the way, as was only natural.
She was a cat. People stopped speaking
to the Ould Fella after that but Mrs Savage never
refused to serve him even though he stopped
speaking to us. There was no need for Mrs Savage
to get adoption papers. Everyone said
we were going to the Post Office for
a holiday. We've been here since.

She said there was a different attitude.
Everyone was throwing away and there
was no mending. She loved walking
or driving in winter but never stopped
to observe for long, *Oh look at the*
*Mountain Ash!* her sigh went up as she
booted past in the Mini or maybe I wasn't
looking either, only waiting to poke holes
in her snobbery, *Wherever there were*
*Protestants, they planted trees!*
*And what about Spenser chopping them down*
*so he could kill every Gael? You could walk*
*from Cork to Limerick and not meet a soul*
*before the Plantation of Munster! God,*
*you've an answer for everything, haven't you?*
*But I was only just saying!*
*And why can't we have a discussion?*
*Look you can still see the outline*
*of the carriageway at the back.*
*Imagine what we think is the back was*
*the front of the house then...*
She was right about the beeches,
meeting overhead on the road to Mallow –
a green gift from the planters. A lover
of funerals, she preferred Deanes' back
avenue past its heyday with its moss ruff
leading to the neglected cobbled yard,
ruined belfry, *Servants, imagine it!*
The new bungalows were ugly,
*I suppose people have to live somewhere.*
But trees were going to get scarcer because

*The people have gone stone mad!*
*A conservatory, three bathrooms and no one*
*inside in it, where will it end?*
*Sure what about the size of Deanes' House?*
*Well everyone can't be at it and that* is
*the size of it!* Only who gets to decide?
She was the one who, in the dark,
surreptitiously hacked down armfuls
of beech branches and stuck them
in the brown and pink Victorian ewers
she'd rescued from Cotters' farm, they blazed
emerald one summer in our cold salvaged
fireplaces, old was always good in her book.
She was always looking back
and now – me too, rooted,
staring after her.